WILL
TO
LIVE

ROBBY

BY HUGH FRANKS

BOOKS

Will to Live (won an American literary prize, 1980). Foreword by Sir Richard Attenborough
The Point of Acupuncture (Illustrated by Michael Ffolkes)
I'm Sorry to have to Tell You… How to Drive (Illustrated by Michael Ffolkes)
The Longest Night
The Dragon and the Needle
The Triumph of Love and Liberty
The Miracle

PLAYS

Hot and Tot
TV's (won drama award London 1979)
Getting on and off

Film Scripts and short stories

WILL TO LIVE

HUGH FRANKS

Copyright © 2020 Hugh Franks

The moral right of the author has been asserted.

Apart from any fair dealing for the purposes of research or private study, or criticism or review, as permitted under the Copyright, Designs and Patents Act 1988, this publication may only be reproduced, stored or transmitted, in any form or by any means, with the prior permission in writing of the publishers, or in the case of reprographic reproduction in accordance with the terms of licences issued by the Copyright Licensing Agency. Enquiries concerning reproduction outside those terms should be sent to the publishers.

Matador
9 Priory Business Park,
Wistow Road, Kibworth Beauchamp,
Leicestershire. LE8 0RX
Tel: 0116 279 2299
Email: books@troubador.co.uk
Web: www.troubador.co.uk/matador
Twitter: @matadorbooks

ISBN 978 1789018 349

British Library Cataloguing in Publication Data.
A catalogue record for this book is available from the British Library.

Printed and bound in Great Britain by 4edge Limited
Typeset in 11pt Adobe Garamond Pro by Troubador Publishing Ltd, Leicester, UK

Matador is an imprint of Troubador Publishing Ltd

For Judith, David and those who have helped

Foreword

by
Sir Richard Attenborough C.B.E.
President,
The Muscular Dystrophy Group of Great Britain

Nothing surely could be more frightening for a parent than to be told that your child will slowly wither before your impotent gaze and fail to survive his teens? You, I, any mother or father could surely be forgiven for despairing totally in the face of such a cruel prognosis.

Hugh Franks's stepson, Robby, was six years old when the Duchenne type of muscular dystrophy was diagnosed. This devastatingly honest account of the subsequent fourteen years in Robby's life is not a depressing tragedy but a triumphant testament to human willpower and love. Robby and his family do not despair, neither do they ever accept death as inevitable. Instead they fight muscular dystrophy with every weapon they can muster. What shines so unexpectedly from this narrative is the element of suspense and adventure as Hugh, Robby and his mother, Judith, battle for time. Each week, month or year they manage to keep the disease at bay, means that scientific researchers all over the world are closer to unlocking the mysteries of muscular dystrophy.

One day there will be a breakthrough. Hugh Franks and thousands like him live for that moment which, I am sure, must come.

This book is about what happens, meanwhile, about the *quality* of life for those who wait.

Chapter One

The first time I saw Robby he asked me to play games with him, any sort of game would do. He had a football handy, so the game was football. He seemed to fall over a lot but it did not worry him.

'Come on Hugh,' he shouted, 'tackle me harder than that!' He was a six-year-old, full of spirit, with fair silky hair, clever little blue eyes and an infectious smile. At that time I did not know about his parents' unhappy marriage. I learnt about that later from his mother, Judith. I also learnt that Robby was a lonely child. His father spent long periods away from his home in London, fufilling business commitments on the Continent. When he was at home he seldom played with his son. There was a simple reason for this – he had no time for children. To him, they were creatures who were to be seen and not heard, and were discouraged from entering his home. However, he was often heard, for he drank heavily and on these frequent occasions would try to discipline his son by shouts, threats and beatings. Robby would rush to Judith in tears asking for protection from his father. She had tried to comfort and protect her son, and had threatened to leave her husband again and again, but she had never had the strength or courage. She always hoped that her husband might change. However, the Fates decreed that she would be the one to change. She changed partners and married me.

Judith's husband and I had once been old school friends and that was how I had met her. He was a strange boy at school, full of charm, but lacking a sense of humour. He was not easily roused, but I remember occasions when he would violently react to any leg pulling by a quick loss of temper. He was strong and well built, but slow and heavy of movement, so although he presented a frightening physical aspect when angry, smaller boys found it easy to elude his blows. We did not meet for many years, then suddenly our paths crossed in London. The post-war marriage I had rushed into was just finishing in divorce. Meeting Judith and Robby was the change in fortune that the three of us so desperately needed. Her husband's business interests were in Europe, and he spent most of his time there. Within a matter of weeks, Robby and I had developed a strong relationship with each other and Judith and I had fallen deeply in love.

Robby had grown up in the usual way and seemed no different from other boys. Except for a slight stutter, Robby was happy or sad, hot or cold, and, like all human beings, in a constant state of change. He had feelings, sensations and ideas which were often as outrageous as those of other children. But the more his bullying father became obsessed with the need to discipline his son with a Victorian strictness, using the cane frequently, the more Robby and his mother suffered mental and physical hardships. As I was to discover, the problems concerning his father lay deep within Robby and he avoided discussion of the subject. It was some time before a breakthrough occurred, but when it did, it was like the sun breaking through the clouds after weeks of rain.

It had been raining that afternoon as I stood next to Judith at the window of her London flat. We were waiting for Robby's return from school. Any moment now he would be turning the corner at the end of the square. Robby suddenly appeared. He was jogtrotting, not quite running, just ahead of another boy. Robby slowed down to a walk and with both arms outstretched he pointed towards an old oak tree in the corner of the square. They both stopped walking, stared towards the tree and laughed together. A few moments later they began walking again, and Robby played the game of trying to avoid stepping on the lines between each paving stone. As he got closer to the flat Robby looked up and saw us both standing at the window. He waved to us and we waved back. He took a few paces forwards and fell, hard, suddenly onto his knees.

He was standing by the time we had run out onto the pavement from the flat. No harm had been done. Robby was smiling.

'Hullo Mummy, hullo Hugh. I'm all right,' he said, and pointing to his knees went on, 'Look! No cuts, no blood this time.'

'You went down a whopper,' Judith said, 'poor old pavement!'

That night Judith told me more about Robby's lack of muscle co-ordination. His walking often appeared to be clumsy, he had frequent falls. His school had suggested that extra gym lessons might help.

'That might be a good idea,' I said. I'm sure it's nothing to worry about, but why don't you take him for a medical check-up?'

I had to leave London for a few days, but I phoned Judith each evening. On the third evening her voice sounded tense.

'What's the matter?' I asked.

'Oh, nothing – Robby misses you terribly, so perhaps he's a bit of a handful tonight.'

'Shall I have a word with him?'

'No. I've tucked him in. He should be asleep by now... Hugh?'

'Yes... I heard you. I'm still here.'

'Hugh,' she suddenly blurted out, 'I'm frantically worried. Robby seemed to have a lot of difficulty climbing the stairs tonight.'

'Perhaps he was overtired?'

'I don't know. I'm taking him to the doctor tomorrow. His father phoned from Vienna this afternoon. I could tell from his voice he'd been drinking. Thank God he's not coming back for another two weeks.'

'I'll be with you tomorrow evening.'

I did not get to Judith's flat until late. As she opened the door she threw herself into my arms. Tears were streaming down her face.

'Oh Hugh,' she cried, 'the doctor said that Robby has muscular dystrophy!'

Chapter Two

Muscular dystrophy begins so uneventfully that often a long time passes before any muscle weakness is revealed. There are also many types of muscular dystrophies as well as several hundred other disorders which may affect the muscles. Even those closest to the problem may have no idea of the bombshell that will suddenly burst into their lives.

For a while, Judith could not, would not, believe the diagnosis. I tried my best to comfort her that evening, but to make matters worse, her husband phoned again. When she told him about Robby, his immediate reaction was to defend himself – it could not possibly be his fault – there had never been such an illness in his family – it must be all Judith's fault. He could not change his business plans. Robby would have to face his problems like a man and take it on the chin. He added that he would talk to Robby when he got back.

As Judith told me about the conversation, a strong resolve grew within me. She told me more of the traumatic events of Robby's early years. Her parents in New York loved Robby but were over-possessive. She wondered if emotional problems were the cause of Robby's walking and running difficulties. Once, one afternoon after tea, whilst Robby was going up the stairs, he had accidentally smeared some jam, which had stuck to his fingers, on the bannister rail. His father saw the sticky mess and before Judith could intervene, Robby was given a severe hiding. The next day Robby told his mother that he could not climb the stairs. Eventually she managed to persuade him that he could easily walk upstairs, but it took some while for the persuasion to take effect.

We talked on into the night and as dawn broke we decided that we would get married as soon as possible, and keep Robby away from his father's brutality. Robby would have to build inner reserves of strength in the years ahead to help him to have the will to live and survive. In matters of life and death, love strengthens and sustains, and Robby would need much love.

Chapter Three

Like many others all over the world, like many millions of people, neither Judith nor I knew anything about muscular dystrophy. We were soon to learn that there are thousands of people on all the continents involved in the search for a cure, both inside and outside medicine. In Great Britain there is the Muscular Dystrophy Group, presided over by Sir Richard Attenborough. In the USA there is a similar group, whose national chairman is Jerry Lewis. Some of these people we got to know later, but like so many parents of muscular dystrophy children, or of those who have a slowly developing degenerative illness, we did not believe that Robby had the disease. Duchenne dystrophy only attacks young boys, and their muscles progressively waste away. Robby's did not appear to be wasting away.

One of the doctors Judith saw – and we were destined to meet many in the years ahead – thought that Robby might be a spastic child. There were other initial mistakes in diagnosis, which caused much distress and distrust. However, one day a doctor recommended further investigation by a specialist, who in turn insisted that a muscle biopsy was necessary. This involved the removal of a piece of muscle from Robby's calf.

The muscle biopsy is only a minor operation but it does need a stay in hospital for a few days. We both broke the news to Robby.

'But Hugh,' he said, 'why do I have to go to hospital?'

'They are going to find out why you keep falling over, Robby.'

'How?'

'That's a good question,' I smiled at him, 'but I tell you what, Robby – when you come out, I bet I can beat you at football.'

He roared with laughter.

'Oh no you won't,' he shouted back at me.

He went to bed happily that night, but it was a bad one for Judith. She felt helpless, she felt there was nothing she could do. The only hope was that the biopsy would prove the doctors wrong, but she did not see the point of an operation that might satisfy the doctors, but do nothing to help Robby get better.

In 1849, a Boulogne sea captain's son had described in a paper an adult progressive atrophy which he called a 'creeping paralysis'. His name was Duchenne and he was a pioneer neurologist. He was the first to devise a way of stimulating muscles electrically without cutting skin. This enabled him to study muscle contractions and their functions in great detail. He reported that the 'creeping paralysis' first affected the hand muscles, then the arms and shoulders, and finally the muscles of the trunk and lower limbs. Then in 1861 he reported the first findings of the severe childhood form of muscular dystrophy now known by his name. He noted the over-development of the calf muscles.

About a hundred years later I was saying to Judith, 'But Robby looks so strong and tough. His calf muscles are so well developed.'

Like many people, we had heard of polio, and other crippling diseases, but as tragic as those illnesses can be, Duchenne muscular dystrophy is one of the worst.

'By the age of ten,' the specialist had said, 'the boy will be confined to a wheelchair, and by the age of twenty, he will have died, probably of heart failure. During this time the boy will be at risk, because any little illness, such as a heavy cold or a bout of influenza, would greatly worsen his condition. The same would apply if he had to stay in bed with, for instance, a broken leg. He is likely to develop contractures such as a tight tendon in his ankles, and unless warned, an orthopaedic surgeon might operate to relieve him. This would worsen the boy's condition. If he doesn't die of heart failure, he might die of pneumonia.'

The specialist had particularly stressed the undesirability of Judith 'clutching at straws', in the hope that she could save Robby. He had told her that many parents rush around seeking the help of cures of all kinds, all over the world. She must accept that the diagnosis was final and certain – there was no cure for Robby's condition.

For a while the world stopped for Judith. Then it spun again with an endless movement of interpretations, of disbeliefs, and an inability to understand the specialist's words. Why did it have to happen to her son? She felt that there was no justice in the world, only laws – and the laws of medicine were sometimes relentless. No doubt among the other ills, muscular dystrophy also issued forth from Pandora's box. Only hope remained as the best part of our riches. But even hope had been denied Judith by the specialist.

During battles in the last war I was always convinced that I would get through unscathed. The attitude of 'it can never happen to me' is powerful and perhaps a driving force in our lives. It is not only ill health that can suddenly hit us in these traumatic rat-race days. But when any disaster strikes, what then? If we want to survive we have to fight.

As we began to fight the problems, hope returned, and with it the understanding that whilst there is life it must be lived to the fullest, however long or short it may be. And we decided to treat Robby's problem as one of survival.

This, of course, is all very well for an adult, but Robby was a little boy of barely seven years of age. It would need love and understanding, but first a knowledge of the problems involved, for with knowledge it becomes easier to find possible solutions. We were determined to find out all we could about muscular dystrophy, especially the Duchenne type.

The specialist's clinical diagnosis and prognosis was a frank assessment of the physical problems in the years that lay ahead. There is no cure for muscular dystrophy – at the moment. The essential fault lies in the X chromosome, but the nature of the fault is unknown. It is an inherited condition carried by unaffected women and manifested only in males. Sometimes it may appear in a family from nowhere, caused perhaps by a change in the germ cell, a mutation. An affected boy may emerge because he has developed an abnormality in his germ cell, or because his mother has become a carrier by mutation. There is something very frightening about the sudden appearance of a muscular disease by these mutations. However, the chances are very small.

In the last decade of the nineteenth century a German, Wilhelm Erb, classified certain dystrophies. In the process he became convinced that they were all disorders of muscle tissue, not of nerves. These were the forms of what he called progressive muscular dystrophies. Three of them began in early childhood or adolescence and one in adulthood. Just before the First World War, two American researchers in New York, Phoebus Levene and L. Kristeller, reported a biochemical abnormality in muscular dystrophy. This opened new paths for research, but it was not until the late 1930s and 1940s that the enzymes were investigated for the part they played in muscle-wasting diseases.

In the 1950s and 1960s there were rapid developments in the field of muscle research throughout the world. There was the detailed charting of the inheritance patterns of several forms of muscular dystrophy. The accurate clinical features and genetic analysis of the human dystrophies were drafted by J.N. Walton and F.J. Nattrass, then medical professors at King's College, Newcastle. Both these men were destined to become leaders in the field of research. Two Swedish physicians, Kugelberg and Welander, identified a type of inherited childhood spinal atrophy which now bears their names. The American, G. Milton Shy, uncovered several myopathies – ways in which muscles can be affected. In France and Japan diagnostic work was carried out on myopathic processes.

Robby's enlarged calf muscles seemed to coincide with a tendency he had to walk on his toes. Perhaps the increase in calf size is partly caused by this overuse of the muscle. In any event, the enlarged calf is one of the main characteristics of Duchenne dystrophy.

Chapter Four

Robby's first night at home after the biopsy was a difficult one for all of us. The bandages had to be kept around his leg for a while.

As I was tucking him into his own bed, he said, 'Hugh, when are we going to know the result of the Blopspee?'

'You mean the Biopsy. Well, we'll know something in a few days. But whatever the problem we're going to fight it and beat it, aren't we Robby?'

'Of course we are. You've got to help me though.'

I kissed him goodnight, but at the door he called my name again.

'Hugh, do I have to see my father again?' I walked back to the bed.

'Of course....' Whatever my next words might have been, they were not spoken, for Robby burst into tears and cried out that he was frightened of his father. He did not want to see him. He went on and on until Judith rushed into the room and everything became quiet once more.

That night Judith seemed convinced that most of Robby's problems were psychosomatic. Her husband's behaviour towards Robby might have stirred up latent viruses. After Robby's frightening outcry I was ready to agree and we decided Robby should see a psychiatrist.

The psychiatrist told us that when he invited Robby to tell him something about his father, Robby became restless to the point of agitation and verbally expressed his fear of his father. The psychiatrist was of the opinion that the need for prolonged psychological treatment was a reality that should not be lost sight of, and meanwhile it could be very harmful for Robby to continue to see his father.

When Judith told her husband about the psychiatrist's report and that she was finally going to divorce him and marry me, he reacted with threats of violence. Judith, who is American, was also getting pressure from her parents in New York to take Robby there for American medical advice. They too, found it difficult to believe that their grandson had muscular dystrophy, and blamed Robby's father for everything.

The fear of violence, and feelings of anxiety, guilt and blame were not making things any easier for Judith. One thing seemed certain – it was vital to get Robby out of London and away from any violence his father might cause. Judith did not want to go to America, and we searched our brains for the best plan of action. The doctor had instructed me in a range of exercises which Robby had to do every day. Those range-of-motion and stretching exercises were to become part of our lives in the years ahead. We had also been advised that walks and other natural forms of exercise were vital and that Robby should have a normal and stable environment.

It seemed that for the few weeks of summer left, somewhere quiet near the sea would be ideal. I contacted some friends who lived in Wales. Robby was so excited with the idea that it only remained for us to pack up and make the journey. We arrived at my friends' bungalow just as the sun was setting. On this occasion we were not destined to stay long in that beautiful country – but we returned, and Wales was to play an important part in Robby's life.

The setting sun had silhouetted the Carnllidi hill just north of St David's and it did much to uplift our spirits. But it was not until the following morning that the true beauty of this Pembrokeshire corner of Wales made its full impact on our senses.

That first night away from London made me aware of the battles that lay ahead to save Robby. His dystrophy problem was enough to battle against, but in addition there were the deep psychological difficulties to overcome. I slept in the same room as Robby that night and I witnessed a terrifying nightmare that he had in the early hours. At one stage he was pleading with his father not to hit him. I was able to comfort him, but it was a long time before he went back to sleep.

My Welsh friends had twin boys aged eight, Dewi and Geraint. On the night we arrived the twins were already in bed so they were not introduced to Robby until breakfast the next morning. I had managed to start Robby on his exercises before breakfast, for by now his leg had healed. But that first morning made me realise how important it was not to make him feel any 'different' from other boys. Dewi was a bouncy, outward-going, extrovert boy – his brother was more sensitive and quiet. After the introductions at the table it was Dewi who spoke first.

'I looked through the keyhole of your room,' he smiled at Robby, 'and saw you doing exercises with your Dad – why?'

Robby looked at me for help, but before I could reply, Dewi's mother, who had been carefully briefed by us about Robby's problem, tried to stop any further discussion of the subject.

'Dewi,' she said, 'just get on with your breakfast and don't ask so many questions.'

'But I only asked one!' he shouted.

'Robby has a bit of a problem with his muscles,' I cut in, 'and so we're hoping to strengthen them by doing exercises. You could help a lot, Dewi, by doing the exercises with us – would you like that?'

'Yes!' He was delighted.

And so every morning Dewi would appear in Robby's room in time for the 'exercises'. I had already decided that by participating myself, Robby's enthusiasm would be strengthened, as well as his muscles. This proved to be the case, and each morning, the two little boys, dressed only in their underpants, would laugh and giggle and enjoy the gymnastics. It was not long before Geraint joined us as well. Judith remained convinced that Robby had not got muscular dystrophy, and in a way this was a great strength for me. Robby soon forgot his 'Blopspee' and we encouraged him in his belief that he had 'lazy muscles'. It was vital for the situation to develop naturally, but I was determined that everything should be done to keep Robby walking as long as possible.

They were good days for Robby and the twins. Mornings were spent on the beach, which was located in a tiny cove at the foot of the cliffs. Robby had a great fear of water, for his father had once carried him out of his depth and then let go of him, 'to teach him to swim'. There had been a rapid rescue act, but it had left its mark on Robby, for he refused to go more than ankle deep in the water.

It was important for Robby to learn to swim. A disabled person enters a different world in the water. Limbs and muscles which on dry land are dead or useless become alive in the water. They float and are given movement once more. Robby was not upset by only having enough courage to play at the water's edge. Dewi and Geraint, who could swim, would splash and kick water at him, but it was always under control, always good tempered.

For many hours I sat next to Robby letting the waves lap on our feet, or walked with him along the edge of the shore, holding his hand. The temptation to urge him into deeper water was very powerful, but it would have been folly to have rushed at it. One day, the lucky break came my way. We had been walking along the shore on our own, for the twins had gone to the neighbouring market town, Haverfordwest, with their parents. Judith stayed at home catching up with letter writing.

It was very hot and I suddenly felt like a swim. Robby was walking by my side, when I told him to stay at the water's edge – I was off for a swim. I turned my back on him and ran through the water until the resistance of the waves slowed me down. Then I dived into the sea and swam away from the shore. I swam a long way out, then turned around to wave to Robby. Was I mistaken, or did he seem to be further offshore than usual? When I waved to him he did not wave back. I thought he might be wading out too far, and if he slipped into the water all the patient work of weeks could be ruined. I do not believe I have swum so fast before or since. As I approached Robby I could see that he had indeed come out from the shore more than ever before. But that was no longer important – tears were streaming down his cheeks.

'What on earth's the matter?' I asked him anxiously.

'Hugh,' he sobbed and sniffled, 'I want to learn to swim – I want to swim like you do!'

'Well, there's no time like the present, is there?'

As Robby's confidence increased, his fear of swimming disappeared, and with the help of the twins, and inflatable rubber rings, he began to swim out of his depth. His nightmares decreased as the weeks passed, but even with the help of the twins, the morning exercises were sometimes difficult to complete. It was easy for boredom to set in and Robby did not really see why he should do them every day. There was need, for nice judgment, in terms of not overtaxing Robby's muscles.

Although Robby relaxed more and more, I became very concerned about Judith's hopes for our immediate future. She was convinced that the symptoms of muscular dystrophy in Robby were coincidental. All that remained was a rational explanation of Robby's walking problem, followed by a return to London and getting on with life again. I felt that if the prognosis proved to be correct, she would suffer from untold bouts of misery and disappointment. Fortunately, she also knew her husband might appear on the scene in London and that was sufficient reason to keep away from that city for a while.

Then one morning an extraordinary thing happened. I had become used to seeing Robby's enlarged calf muscles. Sometimes Robby remarked on them, but they did not worry him. They had become so much a part of him, that it was not until he was well into his exercises that I noticed any change. I had gone round behind his back to help him with a balancing exercise. I looked at the back of his legs and saw that his calf muscles had almost returned to their normal size. I hid my excitement from Robby, and making an excuse that I would be back in a moment, went to tell Judith.

'Darling! I told you so!' she said, and we both returned quickly to Robby's room.

Dewi had appeared ready for exercises and as we entered he said, 'Have you noticed Robby's legs?'

Robby was smiling and I will never forget the look of total happiness on Judith's face. As soon as the local surgery opened Judith went in.

I had gone to the beach with Robby, and as Judith approached I could tell from her expression that the news was not good. Robby was involved in making a sandcastle, so it was easy to leave his side.

She said, 'It can happen – they can look normal again, quite quickly sometimes.'

'I see.'

'Of course, the doctor is probably wrong. Look at Robby, there's nothing the matter with that boy!'

'Judith,' I tried to reason, 'what we have to do is to concentrate on making his life a happier and more active one – you know that there are a lot of problems for him.'

We were heading for our first serious row with each other.

'I suppose you're going to say next that he is mentally retarded!'

'And you're twisting things to suit your own concepts. What makes you think I'm going to say that Robby is mentally retarded?'

'I just know. The way you look at him sometimes.'

The atmosphere remained tense for most of that day and it was not until Robby had gone to bed, and we went for a walk together, that I began to realise how self-enclosed I had become. My close attention to Robby made me forget that there were other people's needs to be met. Judith knew, with her mind and imagination, that I did not believe Robby was mentally retarded, but her heart swept the evidence aside. I had unwittingly forced a loneliness on her by over caring for Robby. She would never complain about that, but I knew there were times when she felt that I was pushing him too hard. How many of us have the gift sighed for by Robbie Burns, to see ourselves as others see us? Forgiveness was quick on both sides, and I had learnt a lesson on the importance of not being too earnest. That night we also discussed our plan to get married as soon as the law would allow it, although at that time we were not very concerned about bits of signed paper.

As the end of summer approached we began to make plans for Robby's schooling, but no sooner had we turned our minds to this problem, than events overtook us. Our Welsh friends, Donald and Evelyn, had been kind and very sympathetic, but their house was too small for two families. In addition, they had two grown-up daughters, and when they came home for weekends there was not enough room for all of us. Throughout the summer the demand for accommodation was high, but now property was coming onto the market for the winter rentings. There seemed to be no problem about Robby attending the local primary school. He was beginning to develop a slight waddling gait, but the twins treated him as completely normal. When he did fall he was still able to get up without much difficulty, and climbing stairs was only a minor problem. Robby's determination to make his muscles stronger by his own efforts had a marked effect on his morale and ours.

Then we had a setback. One evening, Evelyn had called me to one side and told me of her concern about Robby's influence on the twins. She was understandably embarrassed. 'Judith has enough to worry about, Hugh,' she said, 'so I thought it best to speak to you.'

'Yes, of course.'

'I suppose you know that Robby masturbates?'

'Yes, but I don't believe it's excessive and I suppose it's connected with his inner anxiety. He's got problems and...'

'I know that Hugh. But this afternoon I went into the twins' bedroom. Robby was lying on the floor. He was masturbating with the twins looking on.'

'I see. I'm sorry Evelyn.'

'You'll talk with him of course, won't you?'

'Yes.'

From Evelyn's point of view there was an urgency about the problem, and although masturbation is no longer the dirty word it once was, sexual self-stimulation in the young often produces an unnecessary overreaction. If Robby was doing it openly in front of the twins, it could not be allowed to continue. The next morning produced another drama. Judith's husband had decided to seek custody of Robby. Although we had been legally advised that, in this event, the likelihood of Judith losing custody was remote, it added to the pressures surrounding us. There was no doubt how Robby would feel about having to see his father, let alone be under his custody. Adding to the problems of the immediate future was Judith's doubt about the diagnosis. And then a letter from her parents in New York suggested that to clear everyone's mind of any doubt, Robby ought to see the American doctors. They had already contacted Dr Howard Rusk of the Rusk Institute in New York. He was ready to see Robby at any time. But were we ready to go to America?

I was well into a book about Wales by this time and keen to finish it. This might have gone some way towards replenishing our shrinking bank account. But more important than our financial future was the need to keep Robby on an even keel. Judith was not keen to go to the States, her main objection being the over-possessive attitudes of her parents towards Robby. She felt that they might have an adverse effect on his growing enthusiasm to keep his muscles moving by his own efforts. Yet she was not prepared to believe the London specialist's findings – that she must accept the diagnosis as final and certain. I was beginning to agree with her on this point, for Robby seemed to be responding so well to an atmosphere of greater love and understanding. Perhaps medicine in America was far in advance of Britain. Perhaps their diagnosis might differ. I asked Robby how he felt about going to America for a while.

'How would we go, Hugh? By an aeroplane?'

'Yes, I expect so, Robby.'

'Could the twins come?'

'No. I'm not sure we can afford to pay for ourselves.'

'What about your son, then?'

'No, he couldn't come either.'

'Why not?'

'Well, he's living with his mother.'

'And he hasn't got lazy muscles like me.'

'No. But he would probably love to go to America. Perhaps he can come one day with us, but he has to go to school.'

'Will I have to go to school?'

'If we go to America we won't be there long enough.'

'Let's go then.' Robby said.

'You'll be able to see your grandparents. That'll be fun won't it?'

'Yes. As long as I don't have to see any more doctors.'

'I can't promise that. But if you do, try and remember that they are wanting to help.'

He ran away to tell the twins that we were about to leave for America. He seemed to make the decision for us. There was always the chance that American doctors might have a different approach to muscular dystrophy – if they confirmed the diagnosis. Even after the biopsy, it was becoming difficult to accept its findings. But the treatment for Duchenne dystrophy was particularly puzzling. All medical opinions agreed that there was no treatment for Duchenne dystrophy. There was no method for dealing with it. Physical therapy might delay, but it would not halt the dystrophic process. Some opinions considered that physiotherapy would be wrong in Robby's case. Until he was unable to do his exercises, he should not be allowed to have a therapy that might in any way encourage passivity in him. In addition, he also suffered in no small degree from the psychological traumas of his very early years.

I had noticed that he was reluctant to follow intellectual pursuits. He was certainly behind with his reading and he lacked the quality of concentration. Recalling this period, Robby is quick to admit that he was 'a lazy old so and so', but remembers with pride his interest in Chelsea Football Club. I also remember how concerned we were with his lack of interest not only in reading but also in every aspect of intellectual training. If his disability eventually became severe it would be of supreme importance for him to have occupations for his mind. There were so many imponderables. But whatever the problems, he was an individual with a future, however long or short. If he did have Duchenne muscular dystrophy, we must be determined that it did not 'have' him.

We needed new thoughts and new ideas and the New World might be the place to go to find them. In the meantime, the pressures in England might sort themselves out by totally ignoring them, relying on the action through non-action philosophy.

Chapter Five

On the surface, America does not appear to have much time for the action through non-action theory. Everywhere, everyone and everything seems to be on the move. If to keep Robby moving was to be our prime motive, then America looked ideal. That seemed true enough, providing we did not overdo it. One can keep moving for twenty-four hours of the day, but nobody does it on purpose. However, we were soon to realise that like every other quality of life in the States, medicine, especially research, is constantly on the move.

Judith's parent's, Ruth and Ralph, had been thorough and very active in arranging medical interviews for Robby. He found out about these soon after our arrival in New York and he became very upset. Although I had told him before leaving Wales, and confirmed many times on the journey, that he would be seeing more doctors, the truth had not got through to him. Judith and her mother went to considerable lengths to reassure him, and his grandfather bought him many amusing games to play with. But he felt that I had let him down, that I had deceived him. In the end, I was able to win back his confidence, and although I had not lied to him in this case, I worried about the future. It can be disastrous to tell a child a lie. If he did have Duchenne dystrophy, was it right to tell him that he only had lazy muscles? Telling a child about the nature and progress of a terminal illness is a fearful prospect. It is best not to volunteer such facts needlessly. It must depend on the child's curiosity and his emotional development. Robby always seemed to rely on information from me – he did not seem to expect it from anyone else, not even Judith. Her parents were quick to see this, and it became a constant battle to avoid upsetting them.

'Would Hugh be coming with me to the doctor? Would Hugh come with us? Why can't Hugh come with us?' Robby constantly spoke in this vein, and the use of my first name, and not a family one, understandably upset them further. Robby's grandparents were under deep emotional strains. Even distant relations are worried about the chances of developing neuromuscular illnesses, in themselves or their own children. For grandparents, the strains are often greater. They naturally followed the grandparents' law throughout the world as an established inalienable right, that they shall spoil their grandchildren. This can sometimes be of great value for the grandchildren, for the extra love is often needed. But we noticed in Robby's case that it led to a degree of passivity that was disturbing. Ruth and Ralph agreed that the sooner Judith's husband divorced her, or vice versa, the better. So there was a plateau of agreement, but there were many valleys and hills of disagreement in between. Nowhere was this more apparent than in the way Robby's future life should be handled.

Dr Howard Rusk is a great American physician, renowned for his work in rehabilitation of the convalescent and of the disabled. He is also the founder of the Rusk Institute in New York. He is a man of great compassion and understanding and in some ways an epitome of America – the America that cuts through red tape and gets things done. He started to use these talents in the Second World War, by re-educating the medical thinking of the armed forces, in terms of rehabilitation of wounded servicemen. He carried his ideas and plans into civilian life, and a great moment in his life arrived when the Rusk Institute was built.

A few days after our arrival in New York, I entered the building with Robby, Judith and her parents. We had managed to persuade Robby that a visit to Dr Rusk, and perhaps a few of his colleagues, would finally help him to overcome his walking problems. He did not seem to mind on this occasion, providing I would be there as well, and that he would not be subjected to another 'Blopspee'. But Judith and I felt apprehensive on seeing the number of disabled children in evidence at the institute. Would Robby become depressed and would he relate his problems to these children? Our fears proved groundless and I realised that in the presence of other disabled children, it became much easier to answer Robby's questions about his problems. On first sight, there is nothing more harrowing to an adult than a severely disabled child. But just as black and white children will naturally take to each other, this quality often applies to relationships between disabled children. There are the initial stares of curiosity, but once these are overcome, acceptance of each others' problems often follows quickly. The prejudices and fears of our mature years have not had time to develop. Children are able to watch and listen without embarrassment, provided the level of their development is understood. And to an adult, the degree of distress or over-sympathy can sometimes be dispelled by the disabled child's personality or perhaps by some physical aptitude that suddenly reveals itself.

At this time, Robby was not outwardly showing much sign of a disabled. In some ways, I was more concerned about Judith. The London specialist had warned against clutching at straws. Perhaps a less frank statement might have made her less antagonistic and determined to prove him wrong. But if the diagnosis was confirmed by the Rusk Institute, the effect on her might be doubly disheartening. We did not have to wait long for the disheartening news. After a few hours at the institute we were given confirmation of the diagnosis. Progressive Duchenne muscular dystrophy was quite evident. The progression in the next few years would be extremely rapid. Psychological evaluation revealed that Robby had emotional problems. It was noted that he was happiest when he was free of pressure. I think this applied to everyone involved! The doctors also stressed the importance of avoiding traumatic situations, which would only aggravate Robby's psychological distress.

We had travelled thousands of miles and received verification of the diagnosis, the prognosis and similar advice for a specific programme of action. But there was one very positive meeting with the director of the institute's clinical services, children's division, Dr Leon Greenspan. He was quick to see how well Robby reacted when Judith and I were in his presence. He made the daily exercises much easier in the future by praising our efforts. He made Robby see how much we were all doing to help him overcome his walking problems. He told Robby that the best way he could help us was to help himself, by walking, playing and running as much as possible. He told us privately, not in Robby's presence, that we must do everything in our power to keep him at maximum functional and physical level, so that when a specific therapy was found to stop the progression of Duchenne muscular dystrophy, Robby would be at the maximum of his capabilities in all areas. In other words, he gave us hope. Robby should go to a normal school with normal children, he said, and finally he emphasised the importance of allowing him to live as full a life as possible.

That night Judith was still convinced that Robby had not got Duchenne muscular dystrophy. Her father, a dental surgeon, was convinced his grandson was a victim of the disease. Her mother was too distressed to comment. I felt we all needed time to realise all the implications to enable us to make an assessment of Robby's wants. I supported Judith in her conviction, for this gave me strength – yet, at the back of my mind I knew we would have to prepare Robby for the lean years that lay ahead for him. We did not realise at the time how lean those years were to be, in the strict physical meaning of the word.

Physically, there are two ways in which the boys with Duchenne dystrophy will develop and grow. They either become very fat or very thin. Psychologically, they can become passive vegetables, or they can fight to live and survive and be full human beings within their own capacities. Whichever way Robby would develop, I knew his mind must gain strength to help him fight to live and survive.

We seemed to be beset with a host of decisions, all of them revolving around Robby's future. The immediate problem was where to live. If home is a time and not a place we had no problem, for Judith, Robby and I were happy as long as we were together. Judith's parents felt the wise course was to stay in America, and because of possible dramas with Robby's father, the doctors supported them. At the time it certainly seemed the right decision, and when Ralph rented a house for us on Long Island, the matter was resolved. We moved into the little house in the village of Sagaponack, which is about twenty miles from the extreme tip of the island, Montauk Point.

One of the early lessons to learn about a child is the need to teach discipline. Although Robby was not yet disabled, that time might come, and discipline, a self-discipline, would be of vital importance in his fight for survival. He would need to build inner reserves of strength, especially to overcome certain patterns of behaviour. In addition to excessive masturbation, there was the problem of constant bed-wetting. Judith was worried about her parents' tendency to over-spoil their grandchild. Robby still remembers this time of his life and readily admits that he must have been a somewhat difficult child to handle. He was – but there were wonderful moments for us all, which were adequate compensation. When a success was notched up, it all seemed worthwhile. And it was important for Robby that each new day had its promise of new experiences and triumphs. If he could be given love and understanding, we felt the manifestations of his upset mind might disappear.

Chapter Six

After a short time in Sagaponack his bed-wetting decreased and we began to feel that his life was moving in the right direction. I had been instructed in a new range-of-motion and active assistive exercises for Robby at the Rusk Institute. The doctor had also advised against physiotherapy at this stage. 'Keep him moving' was the motto. Nevertheless, at Sagaponack a few physical problems developed with Robby that made Judith very upset. He was finding it more difficult to balance on one leg during his exercises and he had an increasing tendency to walk on his toes. He could still run quite well, but here again, there was a setback in that he fell more frequently whilst running. Although he got up quickly, I noticed that he often had to brace back his legs and then push on his kneecaps before he could successfully stand upright. I managed to make Robby treat these occasions with humour. Sometimes he laughed so much that it hindered his efforts, but that did not seem to matter, for his laughter made him forget his problem. There were a few tears when he fell on hard ground, for the fall would hurt his knee caps and even cut them, but I did all I could to discourage him from running on hard surfaces, and the nearby sandy beaches proved ideal.

Although it was autumn, the sea was still warm enough for swimming, but too dangerous for Robby. This part of Long Island is very beautiful, but the Atlantic Ocean beats upon its shore. The powerful waves are often accompanied by strong undercurrents, and I dared not risk a return to Robby's fear of the sea. But the numerous inland bays were ideal for children and we spent many happy afternoons at the Hampton Bays. He was able to continue his swimming lessons with me. We began to make friends with the locals and we found a wealth of sympathy and understanding from many of them. Not the least of these friendships was that of Hannah Tillich, widow of the theologian.

One evening when Robby was tucked up in bed, the doorbell rang and there was Hannah. Judith had been in a sad mood most of that day. Her parents had phoned and they were beginning to press for a permanent stay in America for Judith and Robby. They had also suggested that I return to England and come back when the divorce was through.

'Nonsense,' Hannah had said when Judith had told her. 'I know how much Robby needs you both. If you are going to have that kind of pressure, you must all return to England.'

She had the quality of putting life in its right perspective and she was always a great strength to us. We slept well that night and so did Robby. His nightmares had almost stopped, and he was becoming more relaxed.

I felt the coldness in our room the next morning. I went over to the window to close it and saw the snow. There was a light layer of it covering the field down to the Atlantic. I recalled similar scenes in Wales, looking west instead of east. The seasons change quickly in those parts and I began to wonder if we might not as quickly return to England one day. Then we heard the delighted shouts from Robby. He too had seen the snow. It was a happy start to a new experience. It was to be his first morning at a local school, a very expensive private establishment. The fees were to be paid by his grandparents, and the daily break from Robby would give me the opportunity to earn some extra money.

Many authorities believe that muscular dystrophy does not affect the intelligence of the child. We had been told that as there are no muscles in the brain, there should be no corresponding decline in mental activity. Some believe that a confined world could lead to below average mental development. Since muscular dystrophy affects all muscles, some children cannot speak as rapidly as others. A backwardness in forming words could be mistaken for a lack of intelligence. Robby had a slight stutter and he was behind with his reading ability. But the former had already been related to his fears and the latter had an obvious cause. His grandparents had always showered books upon him, with the result that he had become overwhelmed by the quantity. Many of these had been left behind in England, but the house in Long Island was soon filled with books sent from New York. Most of these were picture books which discouraged his reading. Although he would only look at the pictures, he did at least feel a book and turn its pages. I would explain words that might help him to understand the pictures, but he showed no desire to learn their meanings. We hoped that the new school would resolve this problem.

Throughout the world there are good schools, bad schools, good teachers, bad teachers, all of them following old or new ways to educate the young. We had already been told about Robby's school, which was experimenting with new ways – it believed that children should not in any way be driven to learn. Let them arrive at the moment of wanting to learn in their own time. This lack of pressure might be ideal for Robby, and so our hopes were high. I completed the exercises with him that morning in good time and the walk to school, with a snowball fight on the way, got Robby in a very relaxed mood.

I got an editing job with a literary agent near Sag Harbour, but stayed in that job for the same time Robby spent at his new school – all of three weeks. Judith and I became apprehensive about his scholastic progress after the first few days, and Robby now remembers that time with glee.

'That was the most fantastic time of my life, Dad!'

'It might have been for you – it wasn't for us.'

'It was great! I had all that fussing with the doctors. My life seemed to be one continual fight against having those bloody blood tests. Then suddenly I could do whatever I wanted to do.'

'That, Robby, consisted in doing precisely nothing.'

'Well, perhaps that was what I wanted,' and he can laugh today as we recall those times.

Each day after school, he remained silent about the place and would not talk about his activities. I would get back from Sag Harbour and Judith would tell me that Robby was watching television, and try as she might, he would say nothing about school. On the third evening we felt it was time something was said, but first I phoned the principal of the school and asked how Robby was progressing.

'Fine, just fine,' he had said, 'but you know, Mr Franks, I think the boy is a bit of an anglophile.'

'Oh really,' I had said.

'But not to worry, he'll be over that soon!'

I told Judith, and we both laughed.

After supper I said to Robby, 'Would you like to tell us how school went today?'

There was silence.

'Robby! I'm talking to you. Did you have a happy time today?'

He suddenly spoke very quickly and said the words in one breath, 'I played with Plasticine and looked up a girl's skirt. Now can I go and watch television?' I told him he could watch the box. After he had gone, Judith and I stared at each other for a moment and then burst into laughter.

At the end of the third week at the school we decided to terminate Robby's brief but unique experience. He had left the school early, without telling anyone, and walked the two miles home alone, crossing main roads with heavy traffic. The school had not even been aware of his departure. Ruth and Ralph came to stay for the weekend and both agreed it was right to remove their grandson from the school. When we told them of the principal's final words to us, they were even more convinced. He said Robby was not interested in work. A teacher had left a simple mathematics book open on Robby's play area, a euphemism for desk, and he had not shown any interest in it – indeed he had thrust it away. As there were obviously other temptations for the children, we were not surprised. Neither were we amused by the idea of Robby doing what he felt like doing, with no discipline to guide him.

His activity with the opposite sex had prompted me to have a talk with Robby about that interesting subject. However, his obvious lack of interest perhaps meant that he was not ready for such discussions. As a child, I had often been fobbed off with strange and unlikely answers. The stork saga was an insult to my intelligence for I had been given a more plausible possibility by a school friend. This, however, was told to me in the school lavatory with the assistance of a somewhat vulgar drawing on toilet paper. As this was subsequently flushed down the pan, I probably felt that the subject belonged to the field of espionage – it was a most secret matter. I thought it best not to overpress Robby at this stage. Masturbation is not difficult to explain, as, like all children, Robby had found that certain parts of his anatomy gave him more pleasure than others when he touched them. Timing in this matter, as in most aspects of life, is of great importance.

During that weekend, the discussions about the future were again long and arduous. Ralph saw how well Robby did his exercises and he began to feel that it might be better for us to remain together as a family. But Ruth, as a grandmother, found it difficult to accept our way of life. Only husband and wife should live together when children were involved, she said, and she intellectualised at great length on the subject.

I took Robby for walks almost every day. The snow disappeared after a few weeks and an unusual mild spell of weather had come to Long Island. I had managed to make Robby's walks interesting by finding an old three-wheeler bicycle in a shed belonging to our house. Just before Judith's parents returned to New York I had taken Robby out for a combined walk-ride with the bicycle. As we reappeared Ruth came out to greet us. She was always very concerned about Robby taking unnecessary risks, and as we thought that she might classify the bicycle as a risk, we had not told her about it. I had forgotten about this. Robby had been thoroughly enjoying himself, but when his grandmother burst into tears and then castigated me for letting him ride the three-wheeler, he became upset. He did have a slight tendency to roll on the saddle as he pushed the pedals down, but I was always close by his side, and it seemed of great benefit to his morale to propel himself along the side of the road. We had spent many hours together making the machine roadworthy. She insisted that Robby went to bed early in order to rest. When he refused, he was offered various presents. That changed his mind, and he quickly went to bed after an early supper.

There is always the need for an agreed course of action for disabled people. When there is a fight to be won, as in Robby's case, it is vital that those closest to the problem are pulling together in the same direction. Judith and I were becoming concerned about this in terms of her parents' attitudes. Whilst Robby and I had been out, there had apparently been a family row between Judith and her mother, of some proportion. This was completely understandable, for we were all under intense strain and trying not to show this in front of Robby. The argument centred around the best way of looking after Robby and planning his future. There had been complete agreement about a change of school. Robby was to attend the equivalent of the British county primary school located in Sagaponack. But there was a wide difference of views about his physical needs. Whilst Judith and I stressed the importance of Robby doing as much as he could himself, her mother laid greater stress on the need for daily physiotherapy. We also felt Robby must have a calm period of existence. His grandparents wanted him to *live* in New York. Sagaponack seemed more suitable for the most pressing problem, which was to persuade Robby to fight against the terrible odds of the prognosis.

'That period must have been terrible for you, Dad,' Robby said to me recently. 'I remember how much I tried to exploit you! Gandhi and Grandpa always seemed to have a reward waiting for me – that is when I did what they wanted.' Gandhi was his strange nickname for Ruth – when very young it was the nearest he could get to pronouncing the word Grandma. The nickname stuck.

'It wasn't exactly that, Robby. You might have indulged in a hate session against authority, most children do, but it only lasted a short while.'

'I suppose the discipline you *gave* me made me feel more secure somehow.'

'That's why we all need discipline. It gives direction and order to our lives. But I don't think you exploited me as much as you did your grandparents, do you?'

'Maybe you are right, Dad. Say! Do you remember that American football game you took me to?'

That game had done a lot to save one weekend from becoming full of pointless arguments. The first few days at the new school had gone quite well, with one notable exception. Robby had objected to saluting the flag each morning before lessons began. The teacher was very kind and understanding about the little drama, but Judith and I wondered if the omen was good or bad. At the end of the week the teacher told me that Robby could not write.

'What do you mean?' I asked her.

'He just cannot lift his arm or hand enough. Then on the rare occasions he manages to grip the pencil, it doesn't stay in his fingers for more than a few seconds.'

'What happens?'

'He just drops it.'

'He does?'

'I don't think the poor boy has got the strength in his fingers. Do you think that the dystrophy is taking over quickly now?'

'No I don't. Let us work on it over the weekend.'

We were very worried and puzzled by the teacher's report.

I had told the school that Robby had been diagnosed as having Duchenne dystrophy and the staff agreed that he should be treated as a normal boy. His main physical problem *was* still a slowness in standing up after a fall, but the other children seemed unconcerned about this. Apparently he was always helped by one or another child, and in any event it did not happen frequently. Climbing stairs was also a slow process, but he had perfect balance on descending and there was no danger of a fall. These two physical symptoms of dystrophy, difficulty in standing after a fall and climbing stairs, were great worries for us. But we refused to let them take over Robby's life, and he was beginning to respond and fight back with determination. On the other hand, if holding a pen or pencil was becoming difficult, then a very serious physical disability was developing quickly. Judith was certain it was a psychosomatic symptom, and whilst I agreed with her, where was the proof?

Ruth and Ralph had come out that weekend, and Robby announced at the evening meal that he could not hold a pencil in his hand. I was glad he had mentioned it. I had only spoken to Judith about the teacher's conversation with me, and had decided to wait and see what happened. Now that he had spoken about the problem perhaps a cause and solution could be found. Ruth immediately believed Robby, and a long dissertation followed on the need for Robby not to overexert himself. A climax was reached when Ruth went over to Robby and began to cut the meat on his plate into slices. Judith immediately reacted by telling her mother to let Robby cut his meat himself. I saw the flicker of a smile on his face that went as quickly as it came. I said nothing and hoped that the meal would not last too long. Ralph tried to change the subject without success. I came to his help by suggesting we all went to a local football game the next day. Robby was delighted with the idea and Ralph spent some time in explaining the finer points of the American game. Before bedtime, Judith asked me to be the last one to say goodnight to Robby. Perhaps I could find out the truth about the pencil-holding problem.

They had all said their goodnights and I was alone with Robby in his bedroom.

'I'm looking forward to seeing that game tomorrow aren't you, Hugh?'

'Yes I am, very much, Robby.'

We spoke for a while about Ralph's description of the game and we both agreed that it was all a bit confusing. Then I asked him about his school and his playmates there. 'They're OK, Hugh. It's much better than the other one.'

'Why is it better?'

'Because there's always something organised to do.'

'Not like the other one?'

'N-nn-nn-nn-o,' he began to stutter, 'and the tea-tea-cher is nicer.'

We had once been told that muscular dystrophy can produce specific speech problems. The two factors involved are control of the organs of articulation and emotional adjustment. There is a type of dystrophy in which the muscles of the lips are weakened, resulting in distorted speech. Sometimes the tongue is not normal – occasionally, there is weakness in the muscles of the larynx. Looking at Robby so comfortably tucked into his bed made me think that he was very cosy, relaxed – how could he possibly have deep emotional problems? Perhaps the dystrophy was affecting his speech as well?

'Yes, she does seem extremely pleasant and she seems to be very fond of you – can't imagine why, can you?'

He returned my smile and then laughed loudly. I reached for one of his picture books and, sitting beside him on the bed, I read through it with him. These bedtime routines were becoming very important aspects of our life together. He was still reluctant to learn words and was only interested in the pictures. But I was able to train his memory by reciting poems, some of which he wanted to learn by heart. I said some very simple prayers to him and one night he decided to learn the Lord's Prayer. But that was still ahead for us and on this evening I wanted to find out about the pencil holding.

I kissed him goodnight and went over to the door. 'By the way, Robby...'

'Yes?' he reacted quickly. Anything to prolong the time before going to sleep.

'What was the truth about that pencil and not being able to hold it?'

'I couldn't hold it, Hugh. I can't, you know.'

'But you can hold your knife and fork?'

'That's different.'

I went back to his bedside. 'Why is that different?'

'Ppp-ppp-lease, Hugh. It's just different. Can we look at some more pictures?'

'No, Robby, it's too late now.'

'It's not too late to ask me questions, why not more pictures?'

I went back to the door.

'Because, if you want to go to that football match tomorrow, you must get a good night's sleep first.'

I opened the door. 'Hugh!' he called.

'Yes?'

'I was just pretending...'

'About not being able to hold the pencil?'

'Yes. I didn't feel like writing the alphabet. It's boring.'

'I'm glad you've told the truth, Robby. That's the most important thing. It's not a good idea to tell lies. You might start lying to yourself, and then we would all get confused!'

'Hugh. I'm sorry.'

I went over to him and kissed him goodnight again. 'You're going to be fine, Robby.'

'Will you tell Mummy?'

'Yes, I'll tell her.'

'Thanks, Hugh, and I'm sorry.'

'Have a good sleep.'

Judith was delighted when I told her. It strengthened her belief that Robby's physical problems were mainly psychological, and the doctors' diagnosis was wrong. And if she was clutching at straws, perhaps that was a good thing, to make her stronger, more positive, and better able to cope with all the problems that lay ahead. We both felt that Robby's stuttering and his lying about the pencil were caused fundamentally by his deep anxiety state. This seemed to worsen in the presence of people who either wanted to over-spoil him, or those who had a tendency to be too sympathetic. Yet contact with others was as necessary for Robby as for other children. Normal children are sometimes just as likely to become vegetables as those who suffer from physical and mental problems. The same is true perhaps of some parents who have become vegetables. A life of isolation can weaken resolve.

Chapter Seven

A prognosis of death in late teenage years is not unusual. Millions of teenagers have been sent to their deaths in two world wars. But some of them at least had a fighting chance by being well trained. Without training, Robby might be in a wheelchair more quickly. Time does not seem to be on the side of sufferers of Duchenne dystrophy or people plagued by the threat of terminal illness. Yet fifteen or twenty years can be a lifetime. And there is always time for a way of life to be made a happy and active one – in spite of the obstacles along that way.

The vital morning exercises routine continued to play its part in our lives, and at times it was a difficult part to play. Many parents know how children will often delay the moment of physically getting out of bed. If they know that on rising a series of exercises must be performed, excuses not to get up will sometimes flow fast and furious.

'Morning, Robby, sleep well?'

'Morning, Hugh.'

Silence would often follow these few words and I would walk the room opening drawers to take out clothes, pulling back curtains, usually still wearing my pyjamas and dressing gown, while Judith was getting breakfast.

'I don't think I want to go to school this morning.'

'Oh, all right, Robby.'

'You mean I don't have to go?'

'Well, let's see how you feel about it after breakfast.'

'I know I'll feel the same way.'

'You're not feeling ill are you, Robby?'

'No. But I'd like to sleep some more.'
'So would I.'
'Well, why don't you?'
'Because I want to get you started on your day – and Robby, you didn't say this on Saturday. You were looking forward to the football match and so you got up.'
'But today is Monday and it's probably very cold out.'
'Yes it is. But it's nice and warm in here. I'll come back in a few minutes and I hope you'll be up and ready for exercises.'
As I reached the door, Robby shouted, 'I can't possibly do exercises this morning.'
'Be up when I get back, Robby, please.'
Sometimes he would have dressed in his vest and pants by my return. More often than not, he would still be in bed.
'Robby! Come on get up!'
'I think my lazy muscles are getting more lazier.'
'You mean lazier, not more lazier. And I think you're getting lazier, not your muscles.'
'Anyway, I don't feel like doing exercises this morning.'
'Nor do I.'
'You don't have to do them, Hugh.'
'Of course I have to do exercises. Otherwise I'd get flabby and fat.'
'Are you going to do them with me?'
'Yes, I will this morning, provided you're up when I get back.'
I missed the help I had got from the twins in Wales, but doing exercises with Robby often made it easier to get him started. But that morning, when I reappeared, he was still in bed. As I entered and he saw that I was dressed in my pants and vest, he sat up in bed, swung his legs over the edge and immediately began to take off his pyjama jacket. He reached for his vest, and put it over his head and pulled it into place. He stood up, took off his pyjama trousers, walked to an open drawer and took out a clean pair of pants. He went back to the

bed, sat down, pulled on his pants, stood up, smiled at me and said, 'OK Hugh! Let's go.'

Many times I tried to imagine what it would be like not to be able to do those simple physical movements. Robby had got out of bed and dressed himself without any help from me. His movements were not quick, but they were confident, sure. He had done all those things naturally, without thinking, the way all of those able to walk and run do, without thinking. It seemed impossible to believe the prognosis, the idea that Robby was going to get weaker and weaker.

During the exercises that morning, Ralph came in and watched us. He seemed very impressed with Robby's performance, and the presence of his grandfather made Robby feel part of a family effort, a family team, aimed at helping him.

The next muscle examination in New York was again carried out at the Rusk Institute by Dr Greenspan, and it soon became obvious that on three of the tests there was an improvement. The doctor had made very encouraging comments to Robby during the testing and we were excited about the actual gain in muscle strength. Robby was delighted. He was smiling, and all the time making a supreme effort to show the doctors how much stronger he was becoming. He talked about the defeat of his lazy muscles, and remarked that there would no longer be any need for blood tests. He was particularly sensitive to the feel of the hypodermic needle, a factor that was to concern us later in the therapy of acupuncture. No comment was made by the medical staff when Robby spoke about his blood tests, but I hoped he was right in his assumption. His blood testing was always a distressing experience for me, for Robby would at times shake with fear. I would make every effort to divert his attention from the needle, but it was a difficult task. Judith could not stand the traumas on these occasions so she kept out of sight. If blood tests were over and done with, a burden would be lifted from our shoulders.

When all the tests were completed, I left the institute with Robby, intending to take him to a film. But the day was fine, cold, but with invigorating freshness. We went instead to Central Park and he had a happy time playing football. Judith and her mother stayed behind at the institute to get all the latest information about Robby's progress.

The vast majority of Americans pay for medical help and advice – Ruth and Ralph were paying large sums of money for their grandson's medical care. I had not realised until then how much the National Health Service in Britain is taken for granted. Yet no doctor in Britain can earn anything like the money made by doctors in the USA – and in both countries the profession is overworked. The doctors we met in America never seemed to have enough time. They gave the impression of never having a moment to spare, and of being continually on the go. Yet there was always an atmosphere of clinical efficiency at surgeries and hospitals. In the latter establishments there was also an air of experimentation and research. The part a human being, an individual, had to play, seemed to be under-emphasised. But this problem is faced by the nationalised system as well. In any event, our problem, the problem of all people involved in the world of muscular dystrophy and those concerned with degenerative diseases, was to find the right way, the right solutions.

Central Park was the right place for Robby that afternoon. But as we walked along Fifth Avenue on the way home, I thought that his swayback, his waddling walk, looked worse. Yet he did not look tired and he had not overstretched himself. As we entered the brownstone house, the first person we saw was Ruth. Although I was soon to discover that she was deeply upset, she did not show any trace of distress and laughingly asked Robby all about our game in Central Park. When I saw Judith and her father a few minutes later I could tell by their expressions that all was not well. We were due to return to Sagaponack that afternoon, but when I was told the reason for the depressive atmosphere, I knew we would have to stay the night for further discussions with Judith's parents about Robby.

Robby had not improved. Judith and Ruth had been told that the exercises had given him better control of his muscle action. This, coupled with Robby's growing familiarity with testing routines, gave the outward impression of greater strength, but in fact there was no improvement. Judith was very optimistic for she continually made the point that if there was no improvement, there was at least no deterioration. She was equally sympathetic with the impotence of the medical profession in being unable to ease the mental pain and finality of the diagnosis. But she was not prepared to accept the diagnosis, the prognosis, or anything that hinted of pessimism about Robby's future. She was a tower of strength and, in the argument with her parents, needed no help from me. They felt very strongly about the need to do exactly as we were told by the doctors. We had no quarrel with them on that point, but there was so much conflicting advice. It became a matter of choosing what was the best course for Robby. We did not feel there was one right answer to cover every situation or problem, just as there is not one type of child, or adult, or one set of circumstances. I suggested that perhaps we were all in danger of making Robby so much of an obvious priority in our lives that he might suffer as a result. He must be made to feel that although he had problems, so had everyone else.

Judith and I were becoming more and more concerned about the apparent lack of agreement between her parents and ourselves. Although outright war had not been declared, the words used were conducive to an outbreak of open hostilities. Judith was accused of clutching at straws once more, and her parents imagined that if we returned to England we would put Robby into an institution. I have always associated this word with a place of refuge for destitute or infirm persons, with the nineteenth century and Dickens, and Dotheboys Hall, gruel and cruel. Ruth described an 'institution' to me, but I was unable to convince her that I did not believe such places existed in Britain. She told me of parents who dumped severely disabled children in those places and then conveniently forgot them. Except for the occasional afternoon visit, she said, they saw them no more. The children rapidly lost the will to live.

Although I did not blame Ruth for having such firm convictions against these places, I was surprised that she imagined we had any intention of ever letting Robby go to one. Sometimes special circumstances within a family make it very difficult for parents to look after handicapped children effectively. Then they may have to think of a Home to care for them. One would hope that a Home would not be a euphemism for cruel institution.

We returned to Sagaponack full of misgivings and I was particularly concerned that Robby might feel the vibrations that were beginning to upset us. On the way back he had said that he hoped there would be no further need to go to doctors in New York.

'I remember that time so well, Dad.' Robby was looking back to those days. 'It's funny how certain kids stand out in one's memory and others are completely forgotten. The twins in Wales – and do you remember that boy at Sagaponack who said all the English should be dumped in the Boston Harbour again?'

'Yes.'

'But he liked me really. If ever I fell over he always seemed to be there first to help.'

'He was a nice boy.'

'And there was the one from Sag Harbour who said I walked like a Frankenstein monster.'

'He was OK too, Robby.'

'He wasn't really OK, Dad. He used to push me over on purpose sometimes.'

All over the world, boys will be boys, and there is generally a little Hitler somewhere ready to bully the weak. But on the whole, other children accepted Robby's strange walking gait, and the school at Sagaponack kept the children busy. Most of them were too young to have developed prejudices. Many adults found some difficulty in behaving naturally in front of Robby. Some of these were close friends of Ruth and Ralph and therefore knew about the prognosis. There was often an aura of embarrassment and self-consciousness about them. But others did not know the forecast of the kind of future that lay ahead for him. These people were sometimes disconcerted by Robby's sudden stuttering, and if he fell over they would understandably overreact. Judith and I would often talk about this problem, especially in terms of the feelings and attitudes of others. There were some people who were unable to cope with the problems of disability, or any unusual pattern of behaviour, and others who wanted to over-protect, and cut themselves off from others. There was one couple who insisted that the only way to handle the situation in the future would be to send Robby into an institution. They had no children and considered that no one individual has the right to take over another's life. As they were both close friends of Ruth and Ralph we made no comment, except to suggest that they did not make their views known to Judith's parents.

These discussions had the effect of polarising the pros and cons of staying in America or returning to England. We were very concerned about the cost of medical help in America and we felt this would place an unfair burden on Judith's parents. At that time we were not in a sufficiently strong financial position to pay the doctors' bills. In any case, we could see no positive medical benefit for Robby by staying in America. It was becoming more difficult to ease him away from the past and his psychosomatic problems, especially in the prevailing atmosphere of indecisive action about his future, and the constant pressure from Judith's parents, which she felt was unfair on me. The divorce proceedings were under way, and Judith was convinced that life in England, where I had my roots, where my son was, and where we would be able to be together as a family in a less pressurised situation, might be better for all of us. Robby seemed happy enough on Long Island, but there was not enough balance to his life – there were still too many extremes. One moment he could have whatever he wanted from his grandparents. Then the next moment there might be a battle with me about taking things for granted, or for just taking things.

Before coming to a final decision we decided to ask Robby if he would like to return to England.

'Would I have to see my father?' he asked.

It was a long time since he had mentioned his father to me, though he was often in my thoughts.

'No, no you wouldn't have to see him, Robby. We might go back to Wales.'

'And then we would see the twins. I'd like that, Hugh.'

'What about Gandhi and Grandpa?'

'I'd miss them, but they could come and see us.'

'Yes. The problem is whether we should stay in America or not.'

'I don't mind what we do, as long as you're with me, and we can play games.'

Hannah Tillich insisted that to return to England was the best course. As far as she was concerned it was the only course. She urged us to accept from her the expenses involved in going back. We kept on delaying the decision and I was getting more and more restive. I had written to our friends in Wales, Evelyn and Donald. They replied quickly giving details of a cottage close to them which was available for renting. Two letters arrived from my twelve year-old son. He wanted to see me again and when I read his letters to Robby, it was easy to see how pleased he was to have a brother.

'I'll see him, Hugh, if we go back?'

'Of course you will. He'll come and stay with us.'

'Let's go then!'

The night before we left America, Judith and I had a good talk with Robby. I told him that the battle of the muscles was going to be a long one, and this analogy with warfare seemed to please him. He loved to hear stories I told him about the Second World War, of human endurance, courage and bravery. And he agreed to help as much as he could in the battles that we would be fighting together.

America had been of enormous help in terms of giving us advice and strength to battle on. The doctors had wished us well and agreed that they could do no more for Robby than the English doctors. They reminded us that a cure would be found one day, and that meanwhile we must keep Robby as active as possible. There should be no time for despair. Ruth and Ralph did not agree with our plans. They were very upset and angry, but we had made our decision. Friends took us to the airport and as our aircraft turned north towards the Thousand Isles, Judith, Robby and I saw the sun rise a degree on the horizon. A new day had started up again. It was to carry us back, not to England, but to Wales.

Chapter Eight

The voice of Robby shouting, 'Hugh! Hugh!' drifted in on my sleep. Judith was already getting out of bed. I did not want to get up for it was cold and dark, but somehow I managed to say, 'OK, darling, I'll go.'

'Do be quick,' she said, 'he's probably wet the bed.'

I got up and firmly told myself that Robby was having too much to drink before his bedtime. By the time I reached his room, I had convinced myself that Robby's bedtime drink must stop. However he had not wet the bed. He was quietly sobbing.

'Hey, old chap,' I said, 'what's the matter? Bad dream?'

'Yes.'

When I sat down by his side he gradually calmed down. He could not remember his dream, so we were able to talk of happy times. Judith appeared and between us we got him back to sleep.

Later I said to Judith, 'If Robby had wet the bed I was going to insist that he must not have a bedtime drink.'

'But he...'

'It's all right. The old man up in the sky sorted out my thoughts. Suddenly waking up made me bad tempered.'

We had only arrived from America a few days before. We were still adjusting ourselves to our change of environment and catching up on many lost hours of sleep. We had landed at Dublin airport and hired a car to drive to Cork where we embarked on the Cork to Fishguard boat. Robby had enjoyed every moment and it was fascinating to observe his behaviour. On the journey to America he had been a difficult child to handle. Often crying, demanding attention, frequently stuttering and spending time annoying other travellers. On the return journey he seemed to be transformed. He asked questions about the aircraft and the passengers, and he became involved with the whole process and excitement of travel. He laughed a lot, and he delighted us with his funny comments, spoken without a stutter. We began to think that perhaps we were winning one of the first battles, that of gaining Robby's confidence and trust and giving him a sense of security.

Our departure had not been an easy one, so Robby's improved behaviour raised our spirits. Ruth and Ralph had been determined in their efforts to split our little family group. With the benefit of hindsight it is easy to see one's own faults, and as grandparents they were entitled to their views. But we had to do what we thought was right at that time. We left America as we had gone to America, hurriedly. But for myself, there were many regrets at leaving. There was so much more I wanted to discover in and on that continent. I still want to find out for myself why the British in general say, 'I'd love to visit America, but I'd hate to live there.' Do the Americans, in general, say the same about us? Perhaps it will always remain caviare to the general – good things in both the new and the old, unappreciated by the ignorant.

But Wales is Wales, part of Great Britain, or is it? As an Englishman I went to live there with Judith and Robby, with many of my countrymen's prejudices about Wales. The Welsh are not to be trusted – they only look after their own. They are a sly race, let them get on with their nationalism, and get out of Britain. Such harmful preconceptions may lie deep within us and have strong religious foundations. As the power of the English kings made itself felt more and more, the Welsh churches gradually fell into communion with the English churches. Canterbury began to dominate. The Welsh church maintained a precarious independence until after the Norman Conquest, but as the Norman bishops intruded into each Welsh sea, the ancient Welsh church fully merged with that of England, and Canterbury ruled completely. Today, the battle is nationalism and rebirth of the Welsh language. There is an intense love of individualism in Wales and in its people.

We were living in a cottage not far from the smallest city in Britain, St David's. In the cathedral is the shrine of St David and it has become the chief place of pilgrimage for all true Welshmen. But we did not feel foreigners, and as Duchenne dystrophy tried to destroy more of Robby's body, so did our neighbours rally more to help.

Our cottage was in a little hamlet about one and a half miles south-east of St David's, called Trelerwr. Robby's room looked out across St Bride's Bay and on a clear day we could see the Island of Skomer in the distance. A 200-yard walk took us down to the little bay of Carreg-y-Barcud, and twice that distance to the twins' bungalow. Whenever the weather allowed, we walked and walked. Sometimes I would take Robby to the great Whitesands Bay, north-west of St David's, where he would jogtrot along the sand. We lived very close to nature and Robby became familiar with all the types of birds – there were the land creatures, the owls and buzzards, and out at sea, the gannets, which dropped like arrows into the water after their prey. There were the strange-looking cormorants and shags, the curlew, with its sad musical cry and long curved bill. And always gulls – the common gull, the herring gull, and the largest of them all, the great black-backed gull. One of these graceful and strong birds became a close friend and Robby decided to name him Gwillam – perhaps he was a she? We never knew, but we got to know his special cry of 'agh agh' and he would take bread from Robby's hand and we would call to him, 'Gwillam! Gwillam!', and he would fly down to us.

The first poem Robby learnt by heart had to be *Sea Fever*, and it marked a big breakthrough in the training of his memory. By becoming totally involved with Robby in all his activities out of school, I unconsciously began to build the final foundations of our relationship.

'But I can't possibly learn that poem!' he had said.
'How do you think Gwillam would feel about that?'
'Nothing. Seagulls can't feel.'
'Of course they can. Anyway, I don't know the poem by heart, so I'm going to learn it before you do.'
'You're older than me, Hugh. That's not fair.'
'But the younger you are, the easier it is to learn.'

The next day he had learnt the second verse by heart. 'I like that one, Hugh,' and he recited the last line with relish, '"And the flung spray and the blown spume and the seagulls crying!" Gwillam crying!' he added quickly.

I have always believed that anyone who wishes to live fully, needs and seeks poetry. Having once experienced a poem, the reader can absorb the experience and continue to feel it always. Robby was sensitive to the sounds of words – it could only be a matter of time before he would be reading and learning for the pleasure of those activities. Somewhere there was a key that would unlock the door.

His nightmares seemed to vanish and the regularity of bed-wetting changed its course. Before Trelerwr, Judith often had the extra chore of washing sheets and pyjamas, and there was also the disturbance involved in terms of interrupted sleep. After a few weeks in Wales, Robby's bed was more often dry than wet. This was a wonderful improvement, and Judith became more optimistic than ever before. But I was still very concerned about Robby's masturbation. Evelyn was always worried about a repetition in front of her children. But the cause and cure were not far away.

We spent a very happy Christmas at Trelerwr, for in addition to the twins and their family, there was also a small farm close by. There were no children on the farm, but the hard-working farmer and his two grown-up daughters were uncomplicated about Robby and his strange walking pattern. They took him as they found him, naturally, without any fuss, and they let him help in a small way with the animals. The local doctor was kind, understanding and helpful. Dr Middleton worked from St David's, and he was the first to suggest that Robby be sent to the county primary school at Carnhedryn. The twins went to the same school and Robby looked forward to his first day. He was delighted when I told him that he would not have to salute the Welsh flag, but apprehensive about the possibility of learning the Welsh language.

Robby was finding it more difficult to get up when he had fallen over. It was always a painful experience to watch him get up, and for Judith, at times, it became unbearable. She would rush over to him and raise him to his feet. Although this was sometimes necessary, in order to prevent overexertion, Judith began to help so often that there was a danger of her becoming overprotective. In fact, Robby would make no effort to get up if he knew Judith was close and at his beck and call.

'Judith, please,' I would say, 'let him try and get up himself.'

'How can you be so cruel! I can't stand watching him try – you don't know what it's like to be a mother!'

This kind of conversation was rare but it did occur, and if Robby was in earshot he would be quick to exploit the situation.

'Come on, Robby, you can do it yourself, can't you?' But the meaning of my words would be cleverly twisted and changed by him.

'I can't get up myself, Hugh, can I?'

'Yes if you try!'

'But you heard Mummy! She said I can't.'

'She didn't, Robby. She said she hates watching you try.'

'Anyway, Hugh, I can't, so that's that! And you're not my father! You can't tell me what to do!'

Judith would then come to my defence, and once a little drama produced an exchange of words that gave me strength. There had been a similar scene and Robby had again said that as I was not his father, I had no right to tell him what to do.

'He has every right, Robby,' said Judith. 'He has the right because he loves you – and that's more important than anything else.'

Nonetheless, it was becoming important to allow myself breaks from Robby, even if they were only a few hours each day. Such breaks were necessary for all of us, and I needed the time, not only to work, but also to retain perspective. Robby needed it too, for no human being can bear the strain of another's full attention all the time. I found that it was essential for me to have solitude from time to time. Judith was quick to sense this in our early relationship. It is sometimes important to be alone, and even a young boy should be encouraged to find himself. That was the reason why, on my walks with Robby, I would sometimes let him wander in a direction away from myself. I could only do this with safety on the sandy beaches, and one afternoon after school, we went home via Whitesands Bay, where we had such a walk.

It was a cold day but we were both warmly dressed and I was determined that Robby should stretch his legs after his day in school. The tide was out but the wind from the west was fresh, making the sea spray blow in our faces. He wandered away from me towards some rocks where we sometimes collected mussels, and Judith would cook us a cheap but delicious Moules Mariniere. He seemed to be safe and happy, so I wandered down towards the sea's edge. On the way I turned to look at Robby and saw he was waving to me. He wanted me to go back to him for some reason, but I shouted that I wanted to go to the sea's edge first. I walked on towards the sea and a few minutes later turned around again. Robby had fallen over, and he was slowly getting up. Halfway to his feet, he fell again, and I ran back quickly to his side.

He was smiling and thanked me. Then he suddenly said, 'Hugh, I've got something I want to tell you.'

He looked quite relaxed, which made the next quarter of an hour even more momentous, for he was able to lift a great weight from his mind. Perhaps it was on that Welsh beach that he really began to battle against giving in to Duchenne dystrophy. It certainly marked the beginning of a great determination in Robby to battle against all the odds. For a moment the sound of the wind made me think that I had perhaps mistaken his words, but I quickly realised that I had not misheard him.

He repeated them to me, 'One night my father told me to play with myself.'

In order to help Robby overcome his excessive masturbation, I had found that a light approach to this problem seemed to suit the situation. Although he had never before used the words, 'play with myself', I sometimes used the phrase to him, when referring to masturbation. We never dwelt on the subject at length, but I was somewhat shattered by what he had just told me. I felt I had to find out if he was telling me the truth. My first reaction was of disbelief and I put my arms around his shoulders and we headed back towards the car. Normally the twins would have been with us, for their parents shared with us the delivery and collection of the children, but on this day they had taken the bus into Haverfordwest to meet their mother. Robby and I were therefore alone, and inside the car I was able to dig into his mind a little deeper.

'Would you like to talk about it some more, Robby?' I asked him.

'He told me to play with myself.'

'Who was "he"?'

'My father.'

'Can you remember when this happened, Robby?'

'Sometimes at night, when I was in bed. He said to me that if I ever worried too much about anything it would help me to, ttt... tooo do that.'

'To play with yourself?'

'Yes.'

'That was an eccentric thing to do.'

'Eccentric? What does that mean, Hugh?'

'Odd. Strange. And not very likely that...'

'Don't you believe me! He ddd-dd-ddid, and he did it tttttt-to me.'

How would a doctor or psychiatrist have handled this? On the way home, we spoke about school and other topics. All the time I was thinking about Robby's father. I thought of my own son, David. A man might need to be very sick to do such a thing to his son. When David had first shown an interest in sex, by asking me, 'Where do babies come from?', I had replied, 'From Mummy's tummy.' There did not seem to be the need to have a complicated discussion on sexual intercourse at that stage of his life. At about the same age, Robby's father had already complicated and abused his son's future. If Robby was to become emotionally stable to fight dystrophy, it was of vital importance to discover if Robby was telling the truth about his father's action. If he was lying to me, he might begin to enter a world of unshared and lonely fantasy. This would make him withdraw even further. By the time I got home, I knew that painful as it might be to her, I had to let Judith know what Robby had said. He walked very badly up the path to the cottage – I wondered if he was exaggerating his swaying walk, and making it appear worse than usual.

The headmistress of Carnhedryn Primary School, Miss James, was the dedicated type of teacher so often found in these grades of school. Firm, but kind, understanding and sympathetic. She readily agreed that although Robby was behind the other children, he undoubtedly had the capacity and intelligence to catch up. She thought that a small amount of homework would help him. As soon as tea was finished, Robby would start his work. It was not always as easy as that, and sometimes it took a while to persuade him to start. But on this particular afternoon, he began to write an essay on 'If I were a bird' as soon as he sat down at the table in his bedroom. When I returned to the kitchen Judith spoke first.

'Darling, I'm worried about Robby's face – you've noticed, haven't you?'

'It seems to be a bit chubbier doesn't it?'

'Yes. It's happened so quickly. Since yesterday. It's not mumps. He's had them.'

'He certainly hasn't got a temperature. Shall we call the doctor?'

'No,' she paused, 'I suppose it could be the dystrophy.'

'And it might not be. It's all that good food you're giving him.'

She had not yet noticed that Robby was, in fact, getting thinner. It was an imperceptible development which I was able to notice first, for I saw his body every morning dressed only in his vest and pants. His swollen calf muscles had returned to their normal size whilst we were living on Long Island. But there were times when I thought the skin across his chest was getting too thin – his rib cage showed through the flesh too much.

'Hugh, darling,' she said, 'you look exhausted. Is it all getting you down?'

'No. I'm fine, darling – don't worry about Robby's chubby face.'

'But I do. And I worry about you, and my parent's letters – and the way in which Robby's father is getting away without paying me a penny. He's got so much money. It's not fair on you, it's not.'

'Judith, calm down.'

'I won't and I'm going to create such a stink about everything soon – you'll see.'

'Judith! Calm down. Please. I think we've had a breakthrough with Robby. A strong one.'

'You do?'

'It was something he told me on Whitesands this afternoon. He may be lying. I don't know, but I'm certain I have to tell you. In case he is telling the truth.'

'What is it?'

I suppose I did my best to cushion the effect of my words, but it was not an easy task. For a little while she stayed silent. I had taken her in my arms. She suddenly broke away from me and began to blame herself. She was convinced Robby had told the truth. She remembered occasions when her husband had taken a long time saying goodnight to his son – his guilty expressions afterwards, that she took for remorse on his part for overdrinking. She knew, she kept on repeating, she knew all the time. I asked how she could possibly have known, that she must stop blaming herself, that it was not the end of the world but perhaps a new beginning for Robby. She suddenly ran out of the cottage, down the pathway to the sea. I rushed up to Robby's room, saw that he was happily working at his essay, told him Mum and I would be out for a few minutes, then I chased after Judith. When I got to the tiny cove, I could see no sign of her. I shouted out her name, but the wind seemed to drown my cries. It was dark and I stumbled over some rocks. When I got up I saw her sitting in the lee of the cliff face. She was holding her face in her hands and sobbing. I gently put my arms around her shoulders and led her back to the cottage.

As we entered the front door we heard Robby call out. He had finished his homework, and as I went up the stairs to his room, Judith went into the small living room and sat by the fire. Robby had not only finished his work, but had also composed an imaginative essay. It was neatly written, which showed another great step forward, for most of the time his writing was nearly illegible. As I read it through I kept on congratulating Robby on the sudden improvement he had made. He was delighted by my reaction, and when he suggested that Judith saw his efforts, I took him downstairs to her. He wanted me to read his essay out aloud. Judith was still sitting by the fire and we joined her, sitting around it in a semicircle. I praised Robby's efforts to her, and then read aloud.

'If I were a bird. I'd like to be a sea gull. I would like to fly over the sea and go by air to Skomer and back again and I could fly over White Sands. And I could get some bread thrown to me and I would catch it. And have a lot of fun flying. And fly over White sands bay and fly over St. Davids Head. And fly all over the place and have a lot of fun everywhere and I can float on the sea. When a big wave comes I can take off and I won't have to be life saved and I could fly over mountains. And I could fly like a good sea gull and if I were a seagull I could do all the things I've said.'

The punctuation and grammar could have been improved but that did not matter. He no longer complained about the impossibility of holding pens and pencils in his fingers. He was thinking, using his brain, happy and proud of his efforts.

Before he went to bed that night I suggested to Judith that we should have a talk with Robby about his father. After his supper, we sat around the fire once more, feeling cosy and relaxed.

'I believe what you told me about your father,' I said.

'I'm glad you do, Hugh, because it's the truth – it is Mummy.'

'Yes, I know,' she said, 'and now that's all in the past. I do believe you, darling. You know that Hugh and I want to see you grow up into a good man.'

'And a strong one,' I added.

'And, Robby,' Judith said, 'I think it's time you called Hugh by another name.'

'What, Franks?' he said.

'No silly. I think you should call him Daddy. What do you think, Robby?'

'Yes. I'd like to call you Daddy, Hugh.'

'Daddy Hugh!' I smiled.

'No! Just Daddy,' he laughed.

'That would be fine,' I agreed.

Later, when he was in bed, I began to read aloud to him, his first 'Just William' book. Those books were to play a leading role in developing Robby's interest in reading. When I kissed him goodnight, he called me Daddy and it seemed to come naturally to him.

What is in a name? The children at Carnhedryn were not concerned about Robby's surname being different from mine, but in a more sophisticated atmosphere it might have an effect on other people's attitudes to him. Judith certainly felt that the moment had come for him to call me Daddy. As the weeks passed she was proved right, for Robby never used the name Hugh again. Overnight, he had dropped a habit that was deeply established in his mind. In terms of making him feel more secure and free from pressures, it marked another step forward for him.

That winter seemed to pass very quickly and as spring approached, Judith and I could feel some satisfaction about our family. The three of us were together, in spite of all the attempts of Judith's husband and her parents to separate us. And Robby had responded in many positive ways to our efforts. His morning exercises were carried out with great determination and his will to make his lazy muscles work better seemed to strengthen as each week passed. Nightmares were now a very rare occurrence and he stopped masturbating.

I had searched my brain for a way to get him interested in reading and the 'Just William' books had come to my rescue. When I was Robby's age, I had enjoyed them and Robby was quick to catch my enthusiasm. I told him how much they had interested me as a boy. I read some of the book to him, and at an exciting part I would stop. It would be time for him to sleep. It was not long before he asked if he could have the chance to read the book to me.

'Will you help me with the words I don't know?'

'Of course.'

Not once did he stutter as he read to me, and soon he was very happy to sit up in his bed and read to himself. I have often thought how lucky it was that the 'Just William' series had not appeared on television. Although Robby only watched the set for short periods, he might have seen the programme, and decided not to read the books. Perhaps the programme would be a spur for some children to read the books. In any event, in Robby's case, the timing seemed right, for he was no longer interested in picture books only. He wanted to read.

When Robby walked there was now a definite swaying from side to side. When he was standing in an upright position he tended to assume a wide stance. As he now says, 'I used to be in the perfect position of a cowboy about to draw and shoot.' He often played cowboys and indians with the twins, and at Carnhedryn he had become friendly with a boy called Gareth. His parents were farmers who relied for the bulk of their income on the potato harvest, especially the early crop. Everything seemed to stop for the early harvest, and even the youngest of children would be in the fields helping. Robby joined the harvesters, earning a few shillings for himself, and for a while, Carnhedryn School became denuded of pupils. Gareth's parents were warm, earthy people. They loved Robby and they took him into their home and their lives as often as possible, and made him feel part of their large family. They had children of different ages, and uncomplicated grandparents, aunts and uncles. Robby spent many happy times with them, helping on the farm, looking after the babies and feeding the animals.

The activities that he shared with this tightly knit family added to Robby's growing sense of belonging. In spite of constant money problems, there was always an atmosphere of hope and optimism in the farmhouse. If the potato harvest was a bad one, there was the chance that a hot summer would bring the tourists. They would rent the caravan and the money from that would make up for the harvest. The need to 'get' did not distort or corrupt their personalities. The children seemed convinced that Robby would be cured of his walking problems. They constantly encouraged him to learn to swim. And that summer, Robby finally overcame his fear of the sea completely. Although we thought it wise for him to wear inflatable arm bands, he would now float on the water and exercise his arms and legs.

Dr Middleton had arranged for a consultant paediatrician, Dr Keay, to see Robby from time to time. Dr Keay worked in Carmarthen and Robby was always given the treat of the cinema, followed by fish and chips, on our visits to the town. They were very necessary, for the dreaded blood tests were again brought into his life. Although the drama was considerably less, the occasion was a strain on all those involved. But they were often a great boost to my morale, for Dr Keay was always pleased with Robby's condition. Robby's previous medical history had been forwarded to Dr Keay, and on the first visit he told Judith and myself that he was half expecting us to bring in a very severely disabled child, both physically and mentally! The doctor's friendly face had shown momentary surprise on seeing Robby, and from then on, except for the blood tests, every visit helped to make Robby feel that the three of us were fighting those 'lazy' muscles.

Robby's muscle tests were carried out in slow, easy stages, but Robby invariably wanted to speed them up. Muscular dystrophics fatigue quickly and need frequent rests, but Robby would have none of this. He moved his limbs without tiring, as if to say, 'This is a bore – come on, stop wasting time.' But at the back of my mind, there was the nagging thought of the prognosis. I had to keep it there, away from Judith and Robby. Even though the symptom of thinness was now evident, Judith had supreme confidence that all would be well in the end. Robby did stop losing weight for a while and began to gain a few extra pounds – much to the delight of Dr Keay. Robby's chubby face had disappeared almost as quickly as it had shown itself. Then it returned for a few weeks and I began to imagine that Robby might develop into the heavy, flabby and obese type of Duchenne dystrophic child.

There were occasional lapses in Robby's work routine, and once, just after we had moved to a cottage near Whitesands, he again declared that he could not hold a pen or pencil. Judith's parents had been visiting us for a few days, and we had had several disagreements. They had showered Robby with presents, and tried to convince us to return to New York. There were some happy moments. We took a trip around Ramsey Island, and Robby was delighted as the seals swam alongside our boat. All the wild sea life in the world was around us, or so it seemed. But on their last evening with us, Judith had a lengthy and tiring argument about Robby's future. Her parents insisted that they knew what was best for Robby, and that America would do much more for him than Britain. If necessary, Ruth said she would pay for all the treatment. Judith explained that it was not only a question of money, and that there was no 'treatment' for Robby's problems. He needed a stable home life, and love and care. They ended by scowling at each other, with enough complaints between them to last a lifetime. Ralph told us that when Robby was flat on his back and unable to move, we could send him to New York where he, Ralph, would take over and look after him. This remark upset Judith unnecessarily.

After they left we returned to the immediate problems, and to Robby's insistence that this time he really could not hold a pen or pencil. We had a long talk, and when Robby realised that I would not take him to the cinema in Haverfordwest, with fish and chips to follow, until he had done his homework, he suddenly found that he could hold his pen after all, and he completed his work in record time.

Chapter Nine

Perhaps the biggest spur for Robby that summer was the moment my own son, David, entered his life. David had just completed his first year at Hurstpierpoint College and was four years older than Robby. For the first few days I noticed a change in Robby's attitude, brought about entirely by feelings of jealousy. David and I had a lot to catch up on, for it was nearly two years since we had met. At the same time, Judith wanted to get to know David, so he received more attention than Robby. David was also allowed to go to bed later and this created even more envy on Robby's part. But once these problems were overcome, it soon became apparent that Robby was delighted to have a brother. The two boys did the exercises together before breakfast, and David soon entered into the spirit of them, by encouraging Robby.

David was a strong swimmer and loved to surf, but he always found time to swim slowly by Robby's side. The two boys got on well together, and by the end of the first week, David wanted to know everything about Robby's problems. He said he would like to help us in our efforts to stem the dystrophy. Robby even suggested that David came to live with us. He was only able to stay two weeks, but by the end of the fortnight it seemed that we had become a close family. It was a sad moment when we said goodbye to David at Haverfordwest station, and the feeling persisted for some days. But there had been a very positive gain. Robby no longer felt that he was the only one – he had a brother who wanted to help him. Judith was strengthened by the relationship, and although he was not with us, I could tell from David's letters that he had also benefited, for they were warm and understanding in content. We did not realise it at the time, but this meeting marked the beginning of a close relationship that was destined to be of the utmost value to both boys.

Meanwhile, the battle continued and the thought of Robby being confined to a wheelchair never entered our heads. We had no time for such negative ideas, for we were too busy helping Robby to lead as normal a life as possible. Part of my normal life had always included a skiing holiday, and one day I suggested to Judith that we should save and plan for one. She agreed, with certain reservations about Robby. He might slip on the ice and fall over, the cold temperatures might encourage him to stay indoors and not take exercise. In falling over, Robby might twist an ankle, or even worse, break his leg. She proposed that we go on our own and leave Robby on the farm with his friends. She was thinking of my interest, and I felt the idea was becoming too complicated, for we did not want, nor did we intend to leave Robby behind in Wales. I began to save secretly for a holiday somewhere in the snow.

It has been generally accepted that there is no pain associated with Duchenne muscular dystrophy. Robby was never in pain, but there were moments of discomfort for him. He was tending to walk more on his toes and to compensate for this, Dr Keay had instructed me in a self and assisted exercise for Robby. I would help him to move his feet in such a way that his heels pressed down on the floor. But the give and stretch of the muscles and tendons would cause discomfort, unless the stretching help I gave was sustained and gentle. I had also been warned that his feet would change from a neutral, forward position, to an inverted one. Once the feet changed to that position he would find it more and more difficult to walk. But his feet remained straight and we walked. We walked on the beaches and over the hills. We jogtrotted together and once we climbed the Carnllidi Hill to the north of Whitesands bay. Behind us stretched the fields of Pembrokeshire, intersected by stone walls. The sky was clear and we looked west. I told Robby that America was over there and then about the Welshman from St David's who had gone to California in the gold rush days. We seemed remote from civilisation. I told him that the rocky and barren Carnllidi Hill was once the principle residence of the Druids. Over sixty miles away across St George's Channel lay the Wicklow Mountains in Ireland. We had been told that on a very clear day the Wicklows could be seen from the top of Carnllidi Hill, but the conditions might only be right once or twice a year.

'Look Dad!' Robby shouted and pointed to the west, 'There are the mountains in Ireland!'

He was still full of the Wicklow Mountains when we got home, and he could not stop talking about them to Judith. He told her about the gold rush days, the Druids, the view of St David's from the hilltop and – could he please take a Christmas present to school next day, for the headmistress, Miss James?

Early in the new year we met Miss James's father, now an old man, but still following his trade, that of a cobbler. But he was a special and rare type of cobbler, for he only made clogs. His workshop was a fascinating place and he spent a long time showing Robby how he made his wooden shoes. Mr James knew about Robby's dystrophy, and he must have noticed the strange walking pattern, but he treated Robby as though he was completely normal. He joked about the odd shapes of some of his customers' feet, and he soon had us all laughing. Robby's feet, and his footwear, were to become matters of great importance in terms of keeping his balance. Mr James did much to ease the problems that lay ahead, for I often referred to him when Robby was having shoe-fitting problems, and we were able to laugh at them together.

In addition to Robby's normal school learning and activities, there was the added task of learning Welsh. Although this might have confused some English children, it was an extra spur for Robby, and I did all I could to encourage his interest in the language. This also helped him to become accepted by the locals and soon he was being invited to other children's homes for tea. We did our share of repaying the hospitality and our circle of friends widened. There was no lack of enthusiasm for other children visiting us, for I made sure that they were always happily involved playing games with Robby. We were so close to the beach that the games often continued on the sands, and one Guy Fawkes night was unforgettable. We lit the bonfire on the beach and the children put sparkler lights in the sand on the sea shore. It was a calm night and the waves gently lapped around the sparkling lights. The faces of the children seemed hypnotised with delight. The naturalness of our life and the discipline we followed were giving Robby the security he needed. Then when all appeared set fair, our lives faced another dilemma.

As the winter had progressed it became more and more difficult to gain access to our cottage. The only road was a *very* unadopted one and it became a mass of mud. There was no alternative, we had to find somewhere else to live.

But although the problem was serious for Judith and myself, it did not worry Robby. In fact, he enjoyed the prospect of moving yet again. We searched without success for a while, then we heard of a cottage for rent at St Nicholas, a small village a few miles from Fishguard. This would take us some miles from St David's and Carnhedryn but closer to the Prescelly mountains, the seed bed of Stonehenge.

Although we had moved outside the working range of Dr Middleton, he kindly agreed to continue as our doctor, though we never had to call on him. He saw Robby from time to time, and like Dr Keay, he was always delighted with his progress. The words varied from, 'He's holding his own so well,' to, 'His remission period is a very long one.' Robby was now ten and not in a wheelchair. He was still able to climb stairs, though I found that he could manage better when ascending with both hands on the bannister rail. There was a noticeable arching of his back when he walked, caused by his need to find his centre of gravity for the upright position. When he came down the stairs there were times when my heart leapt to my mouth, for his balance sometimes looked precarious. But it was important not to show my feelings, yet be ready for instantaneous action to save him should he begin to fall. Over the years he neither fell nor stumbled on stairs, though apprehension gave Judith's and my heart muscles plenty of exercise. The stairs of the cottage at St Nicholas were quite steep, but Robby enjoyed and won the battles of ascent and descent. The routine continued of exercise, work and play. From St Nicholas it was about a mile walk to the beaches of Aberbach and Abermawr. When Robby had finished his homework we would walk to these beaches and light bonfires on them, using the flotsam and jetsam as fuel. The inhabitants of the few cottages we passed on the way became so used to our daily marches that they could have set their clocks by them. His balance seemed to improve and he was not falling so frequently.

One morning in late winter we awoke to see snow on the ground. It began to snow again as I took Robby to school, and when we reached the main Fishguard to St David's road we could see it covering the distant Prescelly mountains. By the time we reached Carnhedryn School it had stopped, so there was little warning of the drama that was to occur later in the day. The snow did not appear to be settling on the road surfaces and by the time I got back to St Nicholas the temperature had risen so much that Judith was convinced that a thaw would set in quickly. The fall had been so light that I was sure I would not be able to use the old pair of skis I had in the cottage. However, by midday the snow had started to fall again and by two o'clock it was settling on the fields and roads. I tried to phone Carnhedryn School but the lines were out of order. I decided that the wisest course was to collect Robby early from school. By the time I reached the school the visibility was down to a few yards, for the snow was pouring in from the sea, and had now reached the proportions of a snow storm. Most of the children had left, and as there was no one going our way, we waved a hasty farewell to Miss James and set off back to St Nicholas.

Robby sat by my side on the bench-type seat of our aged Ford convertible, delighted at the prospect of becoming snowed in. 'That will finish off school for a while, Dad,' he said, and at the possibility of not getting back to St Nicholas, he quickly decided that we could turn round and go back and stay with the twins.

The car survived a hazardous journey on the main road, for although I was driving with extreme care, the strong wind from the sea was buffeting the near side of the vehicle, adding to the danger of skidding. It is a distance of about one and a half miles from the main road to St Nicholas, and as I turned from the main road into the narrow lane that led to the village, I began to feel happier about our situation. The feeling did not last for long. As we reached some high ground a mile short of home, visibility was reduced to a few yards as the blizzard hit us head on. The tyres began to spin on the road surface, so I lowered the engine speed and they gripped once more. But the windscreen wipers were losing the battle with the snow, and as I peered into the darkness, for it had suddenly become very dark, it seemed as though Robby's side of the car had suddenly been kicked by a giant's foot. There was a loud crack as the car spun sidewards and came to a halt. We had hit a roadside signpost. Robby was delighted, excited and unharmed. I had managed to hold him with my left arm so he was not thrown forward on impact. But his active mind was full of possibilities.

'We must not leave the engine running, Dad. A man was poisoned to death from the fumes once.'

'I have no intention of letting that happen, Robby.'

'It's going to get cold, so how are we going to keep warm?'

'I'm about to get out and see what's happened.'

'But look at the snow! It's drifting up all around us!'

'You stay put inside young man and…'

'But supposing you don't come back like that man in the Arctic with the others?'

'Never mind about that, Robby,' but as I got out of the car I became very concerned about our situation. The snow was drifting, and although there was no serious damage to the car's side, the rear wheels were half embedded in the snow. I knew that there were no houses between us and St Nicholas. It would have been impossible for Robby to walk in the deepening snow. Carrying him a mile would have been full of dangers. There had been no traffic on the main road, and in any case, to return by foot in that direction looked even worse. The snow drift behind us was already too deep.

In the past few months Robby's body had become noticeably thinner and although this made it easier to cope with some of the problems, it lowered his resistance to cold. This thought was uppermost in my mind as I got back into the car.

He looked at me trustingly and said, 'Well, Dad, I bet you're going to get us out very quickly. Can I get out and help?'

I told him about the side of the car and the wheels, but I was thinking rapidly about our predicament. I could not leave him alone in the car and I dared not risk carrying him to St Nicholas. By now Judith would be raising an alarm for we were overdue, but I could not see how anyone could get through to us.

Robby began to shiver from the cold, so I took off my sweater and wrapped it around him. He was still in the best of spirits and suggested that perhaps the Royal Naval Air Station at nearby Brawdy would send a helicopter to rescue us. Then I suddenly remembered some old potato sacks that were in the boot of the car. I told Robby that I was going to try and free the wheels of snow and drive on home. In the boot of the car I found the sacks and a bonus – a child's beach spade. With it I dug away at the snow covering the lower half of the wheels, but the spade broke and then I used my hands. Somehow I managed to dig a channel in front of the rear wheels and I put the sacks into the ruts. I quickly got back inside the car, started the engine and slowly, very slowly, let in the clutch. The car began to move forward, then the wheels spun again. I jumped out, pulled the sacks out of the ruts and laid them on the snow in front of the rear wheels. I repeated this performance for about fifteen minutes, and we gradually moved out of the deepening snow onto a thinner layer.

Robby shouted encouragement all the time. We were both determined to beat the battle of the snow. We got over the ridge of high ground and then we saw the lights of St Nicholas. On the edge of the village Judith was waiting. With her was the postmaster and his wife, our neighbours, and others. We got back quickly to the safety and warmth of our cottage. The world was good again, and Robby became a local hero. The village was cut off from the outside world for over a week. Robby and I were the last ones to get into the village.

That night Robby told Judith all that had happened, and it was wonderful to hear him speak without a trace of a stutter. He had become a mentally active human being and he had now experienced the successful outcome of a physical drama in which we had both been closely involved. Perhaps it was not exactly a matter of life or death, but it seemed so at the time. It had undoubtedly provided Robby with a self-respect that comes from achievement for he felt he had given me the spur to make sure we got through to the village. It was his moment more than mine.

Dr Keay and the other doctors both in Britain and America had stressed that all exercises for Robby should be given to the point of fatigue only. One of his daily exercises consisted of lying flat on his back on the floor and swinging his body forward to touch his toes. One morning during the snowed-in period at St Nicholas, I noticed that he was finding difficulty in doing this exercise. It was the beginning of weakening muscle power in his back, which eventually resulted in his body becoming arched beyond normal limits. The warning light of over-fatigue was flashing, so that particular exercise was dropped from the daily routine. But a few days later, when the village was 'liberated', and we could buy fresh food once more, Robby demonstrated how much muscle power his back still contained. The road in front of our cottage wound its way to Strumble Head and we often walked that way. But the snow lay on the road surface enough for skiing, so Robby and I skied instead of walking.

His skiing consisted of standing on the back of my skis and holding on tight by clasping his arms around my waist. Close contact with the ground gives a great sense of speed to skiers, and Robby was in another world. I skied so much that I thought I might finish in that other world. Judith followed, bringing a picnic, and we ate the last of her home-made bread, which Robby had helped to bake. For three days we skied, but then the thaw came and soon it was school again. However, the fates had been kind, for Judith now wanted us to take Robby on a skiing holiday. She was no longer afraid for Robby. How sad it was, she said, that we could not afford one. I had saved enough money from articles I had written, and that night I wrote to David asking him if he would join us on a spring skiing holiday in Voss, Norway. A week later I got confirmation from him that he wanted to go with us, and then I announced to Judith and Robby my surprise holiday plans. No family could have been happier.

Before we left for the Norway holiday, the lambing season started. A local farmer asked Robby if he would like to witness the birth of a lamb, and one afternoon after school, Robby and I were met by a very excited Judith. The farmer's boy had called and told her some lambs might be born that evening. The invitation and the coming event did not excite Robby, but it gave me the chance to find out if he understood the anatomy of living creatures. I had always made a point of answering any questions that Robby put to me about sex. This resulted in questions coming easily to him, and as soon as he had heard about the lambing season, he asked me if lambs made love the same way as mums and dads did. I answered this direct and very blunt question with a simple 'Yes'.

Later that afternoon, Robby witnessed the birth of twin black lambs. He became excited and thrilled as the two creatures came into the world. The ewe was a gregarious animal, for she seemed unperturbed by our presence and appeared to like Robby as he gently stroked her woolly coat. But the happiest moment came for him when the farmer asked him to hold the two young lambs and to give them each a name. One was a boy, the other a girl, and his suggested names seemed perfect.

'Sammy and Polly,' he called them.

'That's the names they'll have then, Robby,' the farmer said, 'and you can come and see them whenever you want to.'

'Oh thank you.'

'There you are then.'

At bedtime that night he asked me about the progress of his lazy muscles. The moment before saying his prayers he said, 'Do animals have problems with walking, Dad?'

'Yes, they can hurt themselves just as we can.'

'Sammy and Polly are fine. Didn't their tails look funny wiggly little things?'

'Yes, Robby.'

'You don't have to be hurt to have walking problems do you, Dad – because look at me?'

'No, that's right. But we're going to get you better aren't we?'

'Yes. But my lazy muscles still don't seem to get more woken up, do they?'

'You're doing fine, Robby. You really are. And, I can't wait to see you on skis.'

He had said that one did not *have* to be hurt to *have* walking problems, meaning of course, a physical injury. At that moment I thought of the injury to the mind. The anxieties and worries that can cripple and kill as surely as physical damage. The emotional stresses that can be as harmful as a virus, a germ or a poison. Robby's *very* early years had been full of traumas, and I wondered to what degree these had affected his physical problems. Nevertheless, he was battling to make himself better. His mind was being healed of past injuries.

Chapter Ten

We arrived in Voss in mid-April, but in spite of the lateness of the season, there was still enough snow for skiing. We went on a package tour, meeting David at Newcastle, where we boarded the overnight boat for Bergen. As the time for departure approached, I began to think that perhaps I was going too far with the policy of allowing Robby to lead as full a life as possible. The weather forecast for the crossing was 'very rough' and I was not the only person to imagine the difficulties that Robby might *have* to face. Just before we cast off, Judith and I were looking *over* the rails of the boat at the quayside below. David had taken Robby on an exploratory walk around the ship. She was a sturdy, sea-going vessel of Norwegian origin, but this did not allay Judith's fears.

'Supposing, darling,' she said to me and then repeated the words with some emphasis, 'supposing, darling, something happens to the ship? What will Robby do?'

'This is a fine time to ask that!'

'It's a better time than out in the middle of the North Sea!'

'What would he do?' I said, 'Well, he'd sink or swim like the rest of us.'

'At least David and you would have a chance!'

'Do you think we wouldn't help him? How many times in the past weeks have we said, supposing he falls on the snow or ice and breaks a leg!'

'Well,' she paused, 'he might just do that.'

We had indeed thought about it many times, but each time we had come to the same conclusions. If we were careful, he would not fall. It would be a wonderful experience for him. And, as important, he would be doing something that others wanted to do – Judith, David, and more especially, myself. We had hired our ski kit in Haverfordwest, and to keep costs down, I would do the instructing. The biggest problem had been finding a pair of boots for Robby. After much searching, an ideal pair had been found, which fitted snugly round his ankles, giving him more support than his normal shoes.

The wind was getting stronger and even though the ship was tied to the dockside, she was already swaying and rocking more than enough for our liking. As Judith and I discussed the improbable happenings, I became cantankerous, and suggested that we cancel the holiday – if we were quick enough we could go ashore before cast off.

'That would be crazy,' she said. 'But you think we're crazy to go!'

'I didn't say that! Oh! Bah! Never mind!'

Something or someone was pushing into my back. I turned and there was David, with Robby by his side.

'It's going to be a super crossing, Dad!' said David. 'Yes,' Robby was quick to agree, 'it's going to be so rough out in the sea. A sailor told us, didn't he, David?'

Judith and I looked at each other. 'That will be fun,' Judith said, and smiled at me.

As soon as we entered the North Sea from the harbour, the full force of the gale hit us. Robby was already sitting down in the saloon and whenever he wanted to move or walk and explore, I took his hand to guide and help him. Somehow or other David and I managed to get him into the engine room. An officer had noticed Robby's walking problem. He very kindly gave permission for him to have a look at the ship's engines.

When we finally got to bed, Robby kept us awake by talking about the day's adventures. David eventually told him to 'shut up'. An hour or so later, he and Robby were sea-sick. It was an eventful crossing.

We stayed at a pension on the outskirts of Voss, and each morning we walked to the cable car. I always made a point of holding Robby by the hand, so that he could not fall. I fitted his skis at the mountain top, where there was an ideal nursery slope with gentle run outs. Again it was necessary to hold him by the hand and I had to ski with some agility to keep by his side, maintaining my own balance as well as his. Sometimes I held him by the waist and took him down the slopes between my legs. He kept his skis on, and we became a familiar sight on the slopes. Whilst I took Judith and David on separate lessons, Robby would watch from a shelter at the top of a chair lift.

In the evenings we played games inside the pension, and one night we took Robby to a disco. He had his first taste of alcohol, danced with Judith, and in the early hours of the morning, David pulled him back to our pension on a toboggan. The boys shared a room and in the mornings they both got out of bed with unusual alacrity. Robby was now a little slower at getting dressed, but he was able to do so without help. But first he did his exercises with David.

During our stay in Voss, Robby was treated as a normal boy by everyone we met. They could all see his walking problems, but they ignored them. Occasionally, when he was out of earshot, we would be asked what was wrong with his walking, but even then the questions were put in an uncomplicated manner. Perhaps the holiday spirit helped attitudes, or possibly there was admiration for our family group in taking Robby. Whatever the reason, there was no doubting the complete success of the holiday. In addition, Robby and David became closer friends. By the time we returned to Wales, it seemed as though we had been away for a lifetime, but we had only been able to afford an eight-day stay in Voss.

We still kept close contact with the twins although they lived in St David's. Robby saw them every day at Carnhedryn, and one day in early summer we invited them for tea after school. About this time, we had been advised that plenty of fish might be beneficial to Robby. Judith had mentioned to Evelyn that the twins would be having more of a supper than a tea, with fish as the main course. Evelyn was most apologetic, but feared that the boys would not eat fish, they loathed the food, and would never eat it. When Judith told me, I persuaded her not to change her plans, but to go ahead and serve the fish. I took Robby into my confidence and told him about the twins dislike of the fish and that we were going to play a game with them. He readily agreed to play it with me. Judith had mixed the fish with rice and herbs and as she served the dish I saw the twins looking at it suspiciously.

Geraint began to sniff it, so I had to act quickly.

'That's a wonderful meal Judith has prepared for you, boys. It's called Gibraltar Chicken. It's delicious.'

'Gibraltar Chicken?' said Dewi, 'What's that?'

I looked at Robby. He was finding it very difficult to keep a straight face, but he was behaving magnificently in my support.

'Oh,' I said, 'it's a kind of dish from Gibraltar. You must try it – go on, take a bite.'

'Mmm!' exclaimed Geraint, 'It's great!'

Evelyn thereafter was ever grateful to Judith for getting the twins to add the necessary proteins to their diet by eating fish. When did the twins discover the truth? We did not stay in Wales long enough to find out, for we were being pulled in other directions.

We spent another happy summer in Pembrokeshire and in the school holidays David joined us for three weeks. There was swimming for Robby and visits to Fishguard Harbour, where, from the quayside, I taught the boys how to fish for mackerel. Once we went to Skomer Island and toured the bird sanctuary. On the way back to Solva, a storm suddenly arose and we were lucky to make safe harbour. The lifeboat had been alerted for us and there was great excitement in our little boat and a lot of apprehension.

We went to the Fishguard Show and Robby had pony rides with Gareth. There were cinema visits to Haverfordwest, with fish and chips to follow, and trips to the Prescelly mountains. Robby was still walking and jog trotting, but he was getting thinner and Judith was trying to fatten him without much success. He still dressed himself but it was taking longer, for raising arms and stretching legs was becoming difficult. One morning Robby suggested that he should be timed whilst getting dressed. His clever idea acted as a spur and the chore of getting dressed became a game. We had a record time for every item of clothing, and for the final total time it took to get dressed. He was thinking much more positively about himself and the feelings of others, and he was growing into a better person.

One day on a deserted beach we found a baby seal covered in oil, and Robby cried, for he thought the creature was dead. But there was life, and I carried the seal home. We called the RSPCA man from Haverfordwest and he took the seal away telling us it would not live for long. Robby cried again, but two days later the man called to say the seal had made a miraculous recovery and would live. Robby was happy again and the little drama reaffirmed Judith's faith, for she told me she was still convinced that Robby had not got Duchenne dystrophy – and miracles can always happen. I had to have the same belief and yet still prepare for any eventuality.

We both felt that Robby's brain was not being stretched enough in Wales. Life for him in the future might depend on his interest in pursuits of the mind. There were moments of setback in this field, and another time, when he announced yet again that he could not hold a pen or a pencil. The problem was quickly overcome after a day of mild 'sanctions'. Discipline, guided by love and understanding was of vital importance to Robby to keep him going, to give him a sense of responsibility and achievement. I had a friend who was headmaster of a school in Sussex, Ted Robertson, of Hollingbury Court School. I wrote to him asking for his advice about Robby's scholastic future.

Chapter Eleven

Robby had always shown great love for animals. He saw Sammy and Polly as often as possible, but they were now out in the fields, although they came to him whenever he called them. He even approached an enormous Hereford bull without any fear or trepidation. The farmer quickly intervened, in case, but there was no doubting Robby's love and trust of the animal. Just before we left Wales, the local farm cat gave birth to five kittens. As soon as Robby saw them he wanted all five, but after much discussion he settled for two of them, a black tom and a female tiger cat. They were destined to outlive their nine lives, and for Robby they became, for a while, a close part of his life. He named them Mee and Oww.

Judith and I began to worry about David. Some of his letters indicated that he was often homesick for us. Within the framework of his life with his mother, there seemed to be a need for him to share some of his life with us. When Judith had first met him, he was shy, and to some extent, withdrawn. We felt it would be good for him to see more of us. It was for this reason, as well as for Robby, that we turned towards Sussex. David was at Hurstpierpoint, and Hollingbury Court School was not far away, in the village of Warninglid. David could see more of us and Robby would see more of his brother.

One day, soon after Robby's summer holidays had started, a letter arrived from Ted Robertson. He wanted us to visit him and discuss Robby's walking problems and his future educational life. It was obvious from the tone of the letter that Ted wanted to help as much as possible. We decided that the long journey to Sussex for a visit of only a few days would be unnecessary for Robby. Gareth's parents, at Tremynydd Farm, agreed to look after him whilst we were away. It was to be the first time since we had met that Robby would be on his own. He was delighted at the idea and I spent some time explaining to Gareth, now aged thirteen, the exercise routine that Robby should follow. I also showed him how to do the elementary physiotherapy he should give to Robby. I impressed upon Gareth the need to see that Robby kept within his capacity whilst doing the exercises, and to take him on walks as much as possible. Gareth's mother promised to keep an eye on them both, but I was very worried, concerned and apprehensive – emotions I did not show to anyone. In the event, Gareth did everything perfectly and Robby was delighted at showing his prowess to another boy, for it took courage for Robby to battle on, especially as he was becoming more aware of his physical problems. Climbing stairs was becoming more difficult and there was always the element of danger about the task of ascending and descending. This kind of thought was uppermost in the minds of Judith and myself, as we began the long haul to Sussex. Could Robby survive in the surroundings of a normal school? One thing was certain, we believed that it was of paramount importance for him to be with normal children and attend their schools as long as possible. A young child does not like to feel in any way different from other children. But the child needs determined parents to achieve this feeling of normality, a determination to deal not only with the 'authorities' involved with such matters, but also with many individuals.

When we got to Hollingbury Court School in Warninglid, Ted and his wife, Maidie, gave us a warm welcome. After they had shown us around the school, they asked me to explain the implications of muscular dystrophy, especially the Duchenne type. If Robby was to have a chance of survival at a normal school, it was only fair to the staff as well as to himself that they fully understood the problems.

'It's a wasting disease of muscles, Ted,' I said to him.

'What does that really mean for Robby?' Maidie asked.

'I don't believe he has the disease,' said Judith. She told them about Robby's early years. They listened sympathetically and when she had finished speaking, we all sat silent for a little while.

Then Ted said, 'Well, Judith, your theories may be correct. Meanwhile, Robby has got this walking problem, hasn't he?'

'Yes.'

'Ted!' I interrupted, 'let me tell you both what it means for Robby at the moment. He is finding it difficult to move his legs, because he hasn't got the full power to use them.' I turned to Judith and said to her, 'If, as we believe, he hasn't got Duchenne dystrophy, he certainly has got walking problems, hasn't he, darling?'

She nodded and I went on, 'Robby hasn't got the full power to move his legs because his muscles aren't working properly. When he falls over, as he does from time to time, it's difficult for him to get up. We have been told that he should be in a wheelchair by now, but he is far from that, so we don't feel in any way helpless about him – just the opposite.'

I told them about the exercise routine and the will we had tried to create in Robby to fight his problem.

'If Robby knew the prognosis,' I said, 'he might have given up the struggle, so he does not know that he has been diagnosed as having Duchenne dystrophy. He imagines that he has lazy muscles that are in constant need of exercise.'

'What is the prognosis, Hugh?' Maidie asked.

'There have been differing opinions about the course of the disease, but they all have the same final verdict. It is very unlikely that he will live beyond his teens. There is no cure.'

'That's if he has dystrophy,' Judith added.

Ted and Maidie sympathised and I began to feel that their school might be very suitable for Robby, if they would take him. The academic record was good, there were day boys as well as boarders, the discipline was on the firm side, but nonetheless fair. But as Ted began to talk about the possibilities for Robby, my heart sank.

'Robby is now eleven, Hugh,' he said, 'and he is probably behind in standard for his age. There are also the physical aspects to consider. The boys here are very active. There are games every afternoon and Robby might feel frustrated at not participating in them.'

His voice went on, and I wanted to say, 'But without trying how do we know Robby won't like it? This is the kind of school where he might benefit enormously from the group spirit, yet at the same time develop as an individual, as a full human being.' Robby needed the rules of such a school, for without rules there could be no freedom. He would learn that discipline and freedom go hand in hand. I already knew that the school encouraged every boy to pursue his own worthwhile interests, without shedding responsibility towards the school and the other boys. I heard Ted's voice again and I exchanged glances with Judith. She did not look very happy.

'... it would not be fair on Robby, or the other boys, if he found that he could not keep up. I have found over the years that if discipline is relaxed too much, it gradually leads to sloppy misbehaviour. I could not make Robby an exception to the rules.'

'Of course you couldn't,' I said, 'neither we nor he would expect that.'

We wanted Robby to be treated as a normal boy. Because he could not walk properly was he to be denied that chance? The world suddenly began to look unpleasant in Sussex, for in Wales there did not seem to be these complications. Perhaps it was wrong of us to move away from Pembrokeshire?

'However,' Ted smiled, 'knowing you, Hugh, and the terrible fuss you would create if we didn't take Robby, and subject to Maidie's approval, I would love to give the boy a chance.'

Judith joined me in the laughter, and Maidie quickly agreed that Robby should be given not just a chance, but every chance.

Ted became serious once more and suggested that Robby saw him a week or so before the term commenced. Suddenly it was all settled and it was not until we were nearly home again in St Nicholas that I began to think about an important factor we had left out of our deliberations – would Robby want to go to Hollingbury Court School?

Robby had spent a very happy few days at Tremynydd Farm. Gareth and his parents had made sure that the exercise routine had been kept going, and they had stressed how keen Robby had been to do them without any special encouragement. But he had missed us as much as we missed him. We had told him the purpose of our visit to Sussex and he was anxious to know everything about the school and that part of England. I told him about Ted and Maidie Robertson and how much he might like the school, for there were so many possibilities to follow – music, painting, a well-stocked library, taking part in plays.

'What about games, Dad?' he asked.

Robby could kick a ball around the concrete playground at Carnhedryn school and sometimes I took him to a level field near our cottage, playing soccer with him on the grass. But his balance at best was precarious. I did not imagine that he would be able to play in team games at Hollingbury. He was looking at me with a sad expression.

'Games?' I said. 'Well, I'm not sure what activities you could take up. They play football, cricket, and they do exercises.'

'Like the ones I do?'

'Yes. I'll certainly make sure you are able to play games with the others, so don't worry about that.'

He looked happier.

'But don't forget, Robby, the world is not full of games players. There are other pastimes.'

'Like school work, I suppose,' he said.

'Yes. But there's pottery and a workshop for carpentry. There is generally something interesting to do outside the classrooms.

Quite a lot of the boys are boarders. They stay at the school instead of going home at the end of the day.'

'Stay at school! They must be mad, Dad.'

'Some of them like it. Perhaps most of them do.'

'I wouldn't. I'm not going like one of them, am I?'

'No, Robby. You'll go there during the day. You'll be mixing with older boys than at Carnhedryn, too.'

'Oh,' he said, 'they are a bit like babies to me at Carnhedryn, now. Well, when am I going?'

'It's not quite as simple as that. Provided we can find somewhere to live nearby, and that you want to go – then we can start planning seriously.'

'I think I'd like to go. Can Mee and Oww go with us to Sussex?'

Our neighbours had looked after the cats in our absence. As soon as they saw Robby again, they purred and rubbed their bodies against his legs.

'Of course.'

'And we'll be much closer to David, won't we, Dad?'

'Much closer.'

'I'll miss here a bit, Dad. But Gareth could come and stay with us, couldn't he?'

'Yes, we'd love that. How much more did you learn about farming from his dad?'

'A lot. He works very hard. He remembers when his dad had to walk the cattle to Haverfordwest for market. But I think he works harder. He gets up very early, brings the cows in, milks them, until their udders are empty. He brought some of it indoors for us to drink every morning. Then he fed the pigs and the chickens – sometimes he killed a chicken by wringing its neck, and Gareth's mother cooked it. Most of the time he was driving a tractor. Gareth and I had a ride on the tractor. He lets Gareth drive it alone sometimes. Then he had a sick cow to nurse better. He was always ready for bed till the next morning.'

Wales, Pembrokshire, the Welsh and the English Welsh had done so much for our boy. It was down there that he became my boy, as well as Judith's. He was a confident, happier human being. He had lived close to nature and unconsciously absorbed the quality of understanding other people's problems. They were the basic problems of survival, of existence, and he was beginning to relate life to his weakening body. His mind was becoming stronger and with it his will to fight his disease. So much depends in life on what is seen when we look – so many cannot look, so many cannot see. Most of Robby's contemporaries with Duchenne dystrophy were in wheelchairs. Although it was getting more difficult for him to walk, he was still walking. Although it was getting more difficult to get up after falling, he could still get up unaided. Like two men looking out from behind bars – one saw mud and the other saw the stars. Robby was beginning to see the stars as well as the mud, and perhaps tomorrow, a cure would be found for muscular dystrophy.

Chapter Twelve

Finding a suitable home in Sussex was not easy, for most of the house and flat prices were outside our income. Is it always the darkest moment just before the dawn? The time for the autumn term had almost come, and we had no home to go to. An estate agent in Horsham had told us that sometimes a cottage came on to the market for rent. They were not always exorbitant in price. Once, when the moon was blue, they were asked to rent a cottage for £6 a week. The moon was not blue when we received a letter from him, but it did contain the welcome news that there was a small cottage available for £8 a week near the village of Cowfold. We confirmed we wanted the cottage by return post, and three weeks later, at the end of the month of August, we left St Nicholas.

David had come to stay and he was a great help to us, for the move had its traumatic moments. It was not good for Robby to remain inactive inside a car for longer than was absolutely necessary. We broke the journey to Cowfold about halfway. With our belongings were, of course, Mee and Oww. Although they had begun to outgrow kittenish ways, they were still very lively creatures. Robby was given the task of comforting them in the car. He did this effectively, by speaking to them through the sides of the basket.

However, they constantly complained about their temporary living quarters, their cries becoming more and more distracting for the driver. Added to this problem, was that of our overloaded car. There was no room for any movement. It was therefore with a feeling of relief that we arrived at our halfway halt for the night. The relief was short lived. Within minutes of arrival, Mee and Oww had not only escaped from their basket, but had also disappeared without trace. I had hoped to stretch Robby's muscles and get him to do some gentle exercises after the prolonged physical inactivity in the car. I could comfort neither him nor David. Everything had to stop until the cats were found. Judith ventured to suggest that perhaps they were already on their way back to Wales. I was not sure whether this was meant as a threat or an encouragement to hasten our search.

By the time the evening meal was ready, there was still no sign of the cats. Robby refused to eat any food, and just when tempers were rising, the waitress in our small hotel rushed over to us and announced that two cats answering the description of Mee and Oww were in the kitchen. David rushed out, followed by a slower-moving Robby. Just as he got to the door Robby fell over. I helped him to his feet and a moment later we were all in the kitchen, watching Mee and Oww consuming large amounts of milk from a saucer they were sharing. Later, when Judith and I were alone, I told her about the incredible reaction of Robby's body at the moment of lifting him to his feet.

I was beginning to discover that it was not always helpful for Robby for me to touch or to hold him in any way whilst he was walking. He was finding it easier to find his own centre of gravity and adjusted his balance accordingly – he seemed to have the natural feel for it. Similarly, I had been advised in America and Wales that the best position for assisting Robby to his feet was to stand directly in front of him. I would lock both my hands around his lower back so that as he rose, his upper trunk was free to sway back and straighten out as I pulled forward near his hips to assist him. If I also helped him when he walked, he tended to hold his upper trunk too far forward. Without the muscle power to counteract the pull of gravity, he could not stand erect.

But in the excitement of the moment, when he had fallen over on his way to see Mee and Oww, I had lifted him from behind in a perfectly normal fashion. Before I had the chance to see if he had arranged his hips and his centre of gravity, he had stood up erect and jogtrotted his way in confidence to the kitchen. Tests were showing that his muscles were not gaining in strength. Exercises and muscle examinations were helping him to control his muscles better, but they would not account for a sudden return of such strength – the strength he needed to get up naturally. The episode was a boost to our morale, for inside Robby there seemed to be untapped sources of energy and strength. Our new home, Clock House Cottage, was built at the turn of the 20th century. It was the rose-covered cottage of story books, with leaded windows and an open fireplace, and Judith fell in love with it. It was the lodge cottage of Clock House Estate, with three bedrooms upstairs, a living room, dining room and kitchen on the ground floor. Although the cottage was near the main road, it was surrounded by a small garden, and the driveway to the main house ran at right angles to our front gate. The garden and the driveway were to play an important part in Robby's physical life. They were both quiet and safe places for him to exercise. There was also a large vegetable garden adjoining our cottage, but its produce was only meant for the main house and the owner, Sir Giles Loder. However, the gardener, Mr Gravett, often gave us treats of strawberries, raspberries, vegetables and flowers. He was a kind, uncomplicated Sussex man of the soil. He often encouraged Robby to keep 'trying hard at those exercises'.

There was a splendid view of the South Downs from Robby's bedroom window, and as the garden faced south, there could be sun in it all summer. But that season was finishing, and it was on a chilly September morning that I took Robby to Hollingbury Court School for the first day of the Christmas term.

The atmosphere of a school inevitably develops from the qualities, talents and personality of its head, and percolates down through the staff to the children. Being a preparatory school, the age group ranged from seven to thirteen, so although, like

Carnhedryn, there were the 'babies', a considerable number were at least two years older than Robby. It was the effect of those older boys that Robby remembers most on that first day and week.

'It was such a different world from Carnhedryn, Dad,' he said, recalling those days, 'what with the uniform and the stricter rules – well, I don't mind admitting, I remember feeling a bit frightened. Then I found out that a boy could be caned if he broke a rule, and I felt even worse.'

'You don't think it right to cane boys, do you, Robby?'

'You know my views on that, Dad – it's barbaric. But then by the end of the first week, I suppose I was semi-enjoying the place.'

'What makes you think that?' I asked him.

'Well, let's put it like this. I seemed to have to work so hard after Carnhedryn, that I had no time to be unhappy! I remember some of the senior boys asking me a few questions about games and hobbies. One of the boarders told me that the food was terrible – at breakfast they had to eat rubber eggs and leather toast. Looking back now it all seems a laugh – and I do remember, there was quite a lot of laughter. One thing, there wasn't any bullying, and there was always somebody around to help me.'

What does it feel like to be a new boy at any school? Robby's reactions were similar to mine. They are probably the same the world over and apply not only to school but to all the occasions when a new life is started. For the first few days at school there is probably more concern about food and being happy. But Robby was 'different' because he had a walking problem, and that first week was a traumatic one for Judith and myself, as well as for Robby. Each morning I took him to school, arriving in time for morning prayers. This meant leaving home around eight fifteen. I collected him at about six in the evening, by which time he would have completed his 'prep' at the school. This admirable arrangement left Robby free as soon as he arrived home for other activities, and prevented arguments about watching television instead of doing homework.

By the end of the first week our worries seemed *over*, in terms of Robby surviving at the school as a normal boy with normal boys. Ted Robertson *gave* a *very* favourable report about Robby's efforts to settle down, but it was not until half term that I discovered how much had been done to make sure that Robby was given *every* chance to succeed. It was then that little stories began to be told and a picture emerged of kindness, consideration, thought for others and an overwhelming respect for the less fortunate from a group of men, women and boys.

The weeks passed, and with them came the winter. Our new doctor, Dr Allen, stressed the need to keep colds away from Robby. During that winter Robby only contracted one cold, which disappeared after a day. Dr Allen was surprised and delighted with Robby's progress, and suggested that Dr Stewart-Wallace, of nearby Ditchling, be appointed as the specialist for medical examinations. I collected Robby early one afternoon and took him to see this consultant. Dr Stewart-Wallace gave him a *very* thorough examination and pronounced Robby in excellent shape. As we were leaving his consulting room he took me to one side and said that it was *very* important not to worry Robby with too frequent medical examinations. Robby, of course, was *very* happy about this when I told him. It seemed that the immediate future was set fair for him.

Robby was able to do certain exercises at Hollingbury Court, but it soon became obvious that he was not able to become totally *involved* in football. However, he was able to play in the position of full back. Although his lack of speed was a handicap, he enjoyed the participation. One afternoon, the master in charge of football asked me to watch Robby play, but from a distance and unseen, in case I put him off playing. It was a great moment for me. The other boys let Robby have the ball from time to time and although they avoided tackling him, they went in close enough to make the game seem real and in earnest. Even from a distance I could sense Robby's enjoyment of the game. Then I threw caution to the wind and went to a sideline. Robby waved to me and seemed to play even better. He fell over from time to time, but he was quickly picked up by some of the boys. The incidents were treated as great jokes by both Robby and the others. It seemed as though it was natural for Robby to fall over. There was neither fuss nor overprotection, yet there was always care taken to see that he was standing erect before the game continued.

Later, when I was taking him home he began to talk about the football game.

'I like playing it very much,' he said, 'but I'm getting fed up with the work.'

'It's important to work as well as play, isn't it?'

'Well, I don't think I want to work!'

'It's not only a question of what you think. Sometimes you must do as you are told.'

'I'm not going to, Dad – so that's that!'

I made allowance for the fact that he was probably overtired and I remained silent. But he continued to complain, so I stopped the car.

'Why have you stopped?' he shouted.

'I don't want Mummy to see a complaining little boy when we get home.'

'I'm not little, and I'm not complaining.'

'That's fine then,' I said, and I began to drive away.

'But I'm not going to school tomorrow,' he suddenly blurted out.

Complaining can become an engrossing occupation, especially when the grumbling comes from a boy about school work.

I had again stopped the car, this time in a quiet lane near our cottage.

'Robby,' I asked him, 'why do you think you're going to school?'

'I don't want to do classroom work!'

'If you feel that, then I might as well say – become a plum pudding if you want to. You will learn Robby, that Hollingbury is trying to instil knowledge in its pupils and to bring out the best in them. That means that you have to study as well as play. And you must learn to give as well as take. You're so much more unselfish than you used to be. Think how those boys this afternoon helped you to play football!'

'I don't care. I don't want to study anymore.'

'All right then, let's call it off, shall we?'

'What do you mean?'

'Let's drive straight back to Mr Robertson and say, it's no good, Robby does not like it here.'

'I didn't say that, Dad!'

'No, but you want to do as you please and disrupt their system of work.'

I had switched off the engine. I re-started it and began to turn the car around to face the opposite direction – the road back to the school.

'What are you doing, Dad?' he shouted at me.

'We're going back to see Mr Robertson.' 'What for?'

'To have a talk with him about you.'

'He'll be too busy to talk to you.'

I accelerated quickly and drove back towards Warninglid. Robby remained in the back seat – silent. I remember thinking that the idea of confronting Ted Robertson with Robby would have been wrong. I prayed that Robby would change his mind before we got to the school. Suddenly, Robby spoke.

'What did you mean by the word "knowledge"?' he asked. 'Developing your mind, getting an understanding of the facts and figures you learn. Information that you can only get from study and work.' I struggled to get a simple meaning of the word and found it was not easy. It had also started to rain and I wished we had gone home, but I drove on. 'Dad!' he called out.

'Yes?'

'Stop the car. Let's go home. I didn't mean what I said.'

'And you'll really work hard at school tomorrow?'

'Yes.'

The drama was over. I turned the car towards home.

Judith and I were convinced that Robby should have the same treatment as the other boys. Yet we had appreciated that Hollingbury Court School had been designed for use by able-bodied children. It was fortunate that all the classrooms, the chapel, dining hall and other necessary places of attendance were situated on the ground floor level. The dormitories were on the first floor. Since Robby did not board, there was no need for him to climb stairs. He was virtually independent of others' help, even when he fell over. He would only be helped to get up if there was not time for him to do it without assistance. The cane was used in very rare circumstances and never on Robby. Discipline was achieved more from a mutual respect between the boys and staff than from a stern approach. But we tried to impress upon Robby that he should not take advantage of the extra help he was given, and that it was of the utmost importance for him to contribute and give, and not only take. He soon developed quite a strong sense of loyalty for the school, and wherever the school team played against a rival school, Robby would pitch in with his voice in support. He would give us lengthy descriptions of the match. It was perhaps at this time the seed was sown for his love of football. His involvement with the game was to become complete in the years ahead.

Meanwhile, Robby's respect for himself began to grow. He became more self-disciplined and better able to fight his muscle problem. The rules and traditions of the school did not stifle the individuality of the sensitive boy. The rules were sensible, and the boys responded to the reasons for them. For instance, boys were not allowed to run in the corridors or passageways, in an attempt to prevent head-on collisions. The older ones were not allowed to go to the village unaccompanied, because of the danger of passing traffic. As opposed to many schools, there seemed to be an absence of trivially pointless or petty rules. And there was a great sense of participation – from the end of term play and the carol service, to the more mundane activities. Every boy had something to do and felt part of the success or failure of any venture. The overall impression of the school was one of an establishment where everyone was trying very hard to give of their best. Good results were always very welcome, but more emphasis was laid on the need for a boy to try his hardest. This was a wonderful spur for Robby, for we had always told him that to attempt well was to succeed. Even though his muscles would not respond entirely to his satisfaction, he knew that he was trying his best to make them work better. Ted, his wife and their staff encouraged the boys to give a helping hand to Robby. Their approach was positive. Negative emotions can fill the blood stream with deadly toxins, which can weaken the body's defence mechanisms.

Robby was attending the school as a day boy. The fees were equivalent to about two packets of cigarettes a day. This was soon to be the spur I needed to give up smoking! But the value of the school to us as a family, and to Robby as an individual, proved immeasurable. It was training Robby to think, and giving him a sense of responsibility and relationship with other normal children.

One night as I was going out of Robby's bedroom, I tripped over one of his shoes and fell heavily. He had got into bed cheerfully, and for a moment he thought that I was putting on an act for his benefit. He laughed and said, 'Now you know what it's like to fall down suddenly, Dad!' I had narrowly missed hitting my head on a dressing table, but I had caught my shoulder on the side of a chair. Robby quickly realised that I had hurt myself, and he shouted out for Judith. She had heard the noise of my fall and was already rushing up the stairs. By the time she entered the room I had got up.

'Are you all right, darling?' she said to Robby.

'It wasn't me! It was Dad!'

My shoulder was aching, but no bones had been broken. We went downstairs, and Judith gently massaged my shoulder. About an hour later the pain had gone, but suddenly we heard Robby calling out for me.

'Dad,' he said as I entered, 'are you feeling better?'

'Yes thanks, Robby, I'm all right now. What's the trouble?'

'I was lying here thinking what I'd do without you. Supposing you had hurt yourself badly.'

'We'd find a way around that problem.'

'It's not nice falling over like that, is it?'

'No, no it's not – how are you coping with it at Hollingbury, Robby?'

'OK, Dad.'

'You like it there now, don't you?'

'Yes – but can we talk about it a bit?'

'Of course.'

I sat down on the edge of his bed and he told me that sometimes the boys would ask what was really wrong with his body.

'What do you say to them, Robby?'

'Oh, nothing much, just that my muscles are weak.'

Was this the time to tell him about the prognosis? Or at least a more detailed description of Duchenne dystrophy than he had known before? For his own sake, I did not want to create additional problems and make his life more complicated. The successive stages of his deterioration might be less distressing if he knew more about them in advance. But how distressed was he at this stage?

'How often do they ask you about it?'

'Oh, not often. Only once really, in the first week.'

'I see. Well, if they ever ask again, why not tell them the same story? Your muscles are weak, but we're trying to get them strong.'

'The doctors don't seem to do anything for me.'

'There's nothing much they can do. They don't know what is causing your muscles to weaken. But they do know how important it is to keep them active. They're trying hard, really hard, to find the cause Robby – many other boys have the same problem.'

'We haven't met any, have we, Dad?'

'No, that's true. But there are many of them. The doctors will find the cause and the cure one day. We've got to ensure that you are fit and well at that moment. Till then, we're going to battle on, aren't we, Rob?'

'Yes. Dad, I want to do a few exercises – now!'

When I went downstairs, I found Judith lying on the sofa.

She was quietly sobbing and when I took her in my arms, she burst into tears.

'I listened outside Robby's room,' she said. 'I heard it all. Oh Hugh darling – what's going to become of him?'

'A man! That's what is going to become of him, darling.' I heard her mother's words echoing in my ears, 'Stay staunch, Hugh, always. Never let Judith or Robby give up.' We all want proof of our words and actions. Actions sometimes do speak louder than words. We had to go on – proving that the prognosis was wrong, but Judith had moments of agonising distress. I did not want her to be alone, but it was unavoidable. Often when she was alone, she became sad.

'He's getting worse, isn't he?' she said.

'A little.'

We both suffered but we did not admit to the suffering. 'Each day is still a new day,' I said, 'and we must not think about the past.'

That night I said some prayers and began to feel better, but we suffered just as much.

As time passed, Robby became weaker. Climbing the stairs to bed replaced his evening exercises. We made a game of the effort he made by timing its progress. Up to the landing took so many seconds, to the top of the stairs, so many more. The seconds turned to minutes and sometimes he would go up on his hands and knees. But he refused to have assistance of any kind, and as his disabilities grew, there was a corresponding increase in his determination.

He was also beginning to find it difficult to get up from chairs. We overcame this at home and at school by increasing the height of the chair he used. Even sitting down had its problems for he would often drop into a chair with a thud. These outward signs of his weakening muscle strength were used as opportunities to find ways and means of fighting the debilitation.

One day, when he found it extremely difficult to get out of a dining chair, I went across to help him.

'No, Dad, no, don't help me.'

Judith and I watched him. His efforts tore at our hearts.

He leant forward with his hands on his knees. He pressed on his knees, pushing them back and locking them. In this way, he was able to get up to a kind of half standing position. With one hand on a knee he then proceeded to swing the other arm like a pendulum. His body went into an erect standing position. I could see that he had to get his back past the pull of gravity, otherwise he would have toppled forward and landed flat on his face. I was ready to catch him, but he had not noticed my readiness to save a fall.

'I did it!' he shouted. He had turned a harrowing moment into one of success. We showed our admiration and relief by hugging him. We nearly knocked him over – we all laughed.

Chapter Thirteen

We began to see much more of David, for he came to stay with us at weekends. On the driveway in front of our cottage I would play football with the two boys. Robby was now only able to play in goal. We encouraged him to give running commentaries on our game and this kept his interest from flagging. He became lucid at the art of commentary and I noticed that there was an increase in the speed and confidence of his speech. This culminated in Robby being given a lesson to read at school during a Christmas Festival of Lessons and Carols. He also sang a solo, one verse of 'Once in Royal David's City'.

'You had a good voice in those days, Robby,' I said to him recently.

'Did I?'

'You sang a solo verse in the carol service at Hollingbury Court, remember?'

'Vaguely – I remember vaguely. Of course there was compulsory chapel too! Though not as much as David got at Hurstpierpoint – I'm glad I didn't go there, Dad!'

'You might have gone.'

'There's no freedom in those places, is there, Dad?'

'It depends what that word "freedom" means. If it means freedom to smoke, to get sloshed, then you're right.'

He smiled, 'Well you know what I think about God and chapels!'

Those many years ago, on the night of the carol service, I had told him that God could not be explained in physical terms.

'He is eternal, Robby,' I had said. 'What does that mean?' he asked.

'He will always be around. On the other hand, our bodies won't. That's what makes it difficult for us to believe in a God, any God. But if we have faith, we can believe that something goes on after our bodies have died. And that something, Robby, is called many names – soul, spirit, it's more important than our bodies, much more, because it goes on.'

'Even when we're dead?'

'Even when we're dead. That's to say, when our bodies have died.'

'How do you know?'

'It has nothing to do with knowing – I believe that happens because I have faith it happens – and I also have a little imagination.'

'Did you think that when you were a boy at Hurstpierpoint?'

'Yes – I think so. But then when I was older I didn't believe it. I went through a stage of wanting proof about everything. And religion doesn't have proof. I couldn't believe anything that did not exist, physically exist.'

'Well, Dad,' he said, 'what do you think happens when we die?'

'We go on in some way – in a way that's beyond our understanding!'

'Don't you think it's time someone found out?'

Children often go direct to the heart of problems. 'You're right, Robby,' I smiled, 'let's work on it, shall we?'

Television helped with some answers, especially the Sunday evening religious programmes. We did not give the media much chance to promote some of its other benefits. When Robby got back from Hollingbury, we spent most of the time playing games inside and outside the cottage. We encouraged him to read as much as possible. The school library helped him to graduate from the 'Just William' books to other authors. Although his grandparents in New York now tended to send too many adult stories, the Nature Library and similar titles were of great benefit to Robby's intellectual development. Though we have never been surrounded by money, we have always been encircled by books. They took up more room than furniture on the occasions we moved. Robby and David were thus able to reach for books of 'all time', as well as some of 'the hour'. Although the former were ignored at first, they were handled and read by them both in later years.

At the end of one term, there was a parents' dance and party. The boys attended throughout, and the first dance they had was with their mothers. It was a strange sight, for the mothers were much taller than their partners, but as the dance progressed it became a very happy scene. The boys had been taught how to invite their mothers to dance with them. Robby came across the floor a little slower than the rest, but he was just as confident as the others when he spoke to Judith.

'Mummy,' he grinned broadly at her, 'may I have the pleasure of this dance with you?'

They waltzed away from me very slowly. I felt very proud of them both.

Another end of term was marked by an ambitious attempt to stage *The Taming of the Shrew*. The producer was Ted's oldest son, David, and the production was a great success. Robby played Petruchio's servant with much aplomb and seemed to give no hint of his awkward walking pattern.

Ted's son David was one of the masters at the school, and in addition to the play he helped to run the pottery classes and gave 'shore' lessons on the art of sailing. He was a very versatile, kind young man, and Robby prospered under his guidance. Duchenne dystrophy often causes mental sluggishness, but by giving Robby a full life and total involvement with normal children, he had become intellectually muscular. But like all children he needed to know where he was going in terms of his future schooling. We had put him down for Hurstpierpoint, and at the time we had seen the headmaster, Roger Griffiths. He was a very able headmaster, having been appointed at a young age after a meteoric rise to second master at Charterhouse.

One of the striking features of Hurstpierpoint is its compactness. All the buildings and playing fields are in the immediate vicinity of the main block. This would make Robby's physical problem easier. The centre of his out-of-school life would be his House, and we chose the same one as David. The housemaster and Roger Griffiths both agreed to take Robby provided he could keep up physically, and pass the common entrance examination. Although we had to follow a 'wait and see' policy, the future plans had been laid, and Robby had the spur of knowing where he was going when he left Hollingbury Court. The fact that Robby could even be considered for Hurstpierpoint was a great encouragement for us all. He was more than holding his own with normal boys. Our love and combined efforts were reaping rich rewards in terms of a young boy's life.

One morning when I was taking Robby to school he began talking about the boarders at Hollingbury. He said how lucky they were, in some ways, to be boarders. They did not have to make a long trek to school each day, and he had heard that they had a lot more fun than day boys, especially in the dormitories. They had pillow fights, told stories to each other after the lights had been turned out, and from time to time they had secret feasts and games of dare. They said the food of course was terrible and of course Robby did not relish the thought of eating it.

I asked him if he would like to be a boarder. After a long pause he answered that he was not sure about it. I did not press the issue any more, for I felt that it would not be right for him or the staff. It seemed wise not to encourage his line of thought, but Judith and I were to be proved wrong.

Chapter Fourteen

Judith's divorce came through and we were married quietly. Her husband did not make any attempts to contact us, or his son, and Robby took on my surname quite naturally. We made new friends in the area, but we began to notice one disturbing aspect about the ones who had children. When they knew of Robby's problem they tended to keep away from us, as if he might be contagious. This created a sense of isolation which was worrying in terms of Robby. We had become a strong family that now included David, but it was good for Robby to meet other boys in addition to those friends he had at school. The other day boys lived a long way from us, and in the holidays the boarders returned to their homes in other parts of the country. It therefore became a full-time occupation during the holidays to prevent Robby from feeling in any way isolated from other children.

We turned to Wales and Gareth. He came to stay with us, and one summer we went back to Wales for a caravan holiday – in a horse-drawn caravan. It was a great success. We travelled through the Welsh mountains covering seven to ten miles a day. At night, we stopped at farmhouses along our route and each morning there was an exciting start to the day. Robby and David were given the task of harnessing our horse, Molly. She was a fine creature, and when in harness was most obedient. The trouble lay in getting her into harness. She backed on us, kicked out at us and terrified Judith. But finally, each morning, we would corner her and she would suddenly become sweet and willing. I always made sure that Robby was sufficiently clear of Molly's tantrums. He loved the animal and spent long periods when we were at rest stroking her. He loved animals so much that he threatened not to go with us on holiday to Wales unless we could take Mee and Oww with us. He agreed to go when he was fully assured that some neighbours would take very good care of the cats.

We all slept inside the caravan and as there was always a stream nearby, we had a swim each morning before breakfast. Robby did his exercises in addition to having the daily swims. He helped Judith prepare the meals and both boys began to appreciate how many of life's gifts are taken for granted. Water became a precious liquid needed to quench thirst as well as to keep our limbs clean. The first job given to David and Robby on arrival at our camp for the night was to fetch water from the farm. In fact, Robby became so concerned by the need to avoid wasting water that he constantly reminded us to use it with care.

When we got home again, the remainder of the holiday was spent between Brighton and Cowfold. I took Robby for long walks along the front at Brighton, and if the sea was calm we would swim. A lot of people tended to stare at Robby, for his sway back was very noticeable. One afternoon, I was approached by a man on the undercliff walk that stretches from the eastern end of Brighton to the village of Rottingdean.

Robby was some distance ahead of me, walking beside the sea wall, so he did not hear the conversation I had with the stranger.

'That your boy?' he asked.

'Yes.'

'I hope you don't mind my asking, but has he got muscular dystrophy?'

'It's been diagnosed as that.'

'He has the Duchenne type, doesn't he?'

'Yes,' I replied and repeated, 'it's been diagnosed as that.'

'In that case there's no need for me to tell you about it. Terrible isn't it? Good friend of mine had two boys, both with Duchenne dystrophy. The boys are both dead now. One died when he was fourteen, the other when he was seventeen.'

I saw Robby coming back towards us. 'I'm very sorry to hear that,' I said.

'The parents were nice people, but they couldn't do anything for the boys. They seemed to hang around waiting for death. There is nothing that can be done, is there?'

'We were told that our boy would be in a wheelchair by the time he was ten. He's now twelve and, as you see, still walking.'

Robby was by my side now and a sixth sense had told me that I need not worry about the stranger and what he might say to Robby. The man had kind eyes.

'Robby, this man says how well you seem to be walking.'

'You really do, sonny,' the stranger smiled, 'I reckon you try really hard, too!'

'Dad helps me,' Robby replied, 'so he tries hard, too. Let's go down on the beach, can we, Dad?'

When I got to the water's edge with Robby and looked back at the undercliff walk I saw the man waving to us. I waved back.

Robby had a purpose to his life and had something to live for. We had tried to involve him in a normal life, so that there was no reason for him to feel other than normal – and many normal people walk in strange ways. It is the way we think and what we are that counts.

It was only a matter of time before we got a dog. There were two dogs at Hollingbury, both belonging to the Robertsons. I was told that Robby frequently played with them. Near Cowfold lived a family called the Colvins. Their two children were too old for Robby, but the parents, Pat and Elizabeth, did much to help us. They told us to use their beautiful grounds for Robby to walk in at any time of the day. Even more important was the offer to use their heated swimming pool whenever we wanted. During the summer holidays Robby spent many of his afternoons in the pool. One afternoon he saw another bather who only had one leg. The other had been amputated from the hip as a result of a war wound. The man, Michael Stephen, was a strong swimmer and did much to encourage Robby in the water. Michael's wife was slowly dying of multiple sclerosis, and within a few years he was to die of cancer. Whilst we lived at Cowfold, the courage of this man and his wife was a powerful inspiration for Robby.

One afternoon, Michael announced that a litter of puppies had been born to the Colvins' cream labrador. Robby, David and I rushed to the kennels of the house and there we saw the still blind puppies crawling around their mother. Pat Colvin came over to Robby.

'Would you like one of those?' he asked Robby.

It was the most unnecessary question of the year and a month or so later we took delivery of our labrador dog, Simon. There were some traumatic weeks ahead as Mee and Oww battled against an enemy of cats. In the end, all was well and the animals accepted the right to coexist in peace without trying to kill each other. Life can be as precious in the domestic animal world as it is in the human.

Chapter Fifteen

I was constantly looking for ways and means of keeping Robby physically active, and in particular of sustaining his keenness and enthusiasm for exercise. The social services suddenly produced a magnificent three-wheeler bicycle for him. This was a moment of inspiration on the part of a government official. This man had visited me one day and asked if there was anything his department could do to help Robby. With all its shortcomings, there are times when British bureaucracy can become very human. We have often found this so – especially when the bureaucrat is treated courteously.

I had told the man how slowly Robby now walked.

'He couldn't manage a bicycle,' the man had said, 'but how about a three-wheeler?'

A medical certificate from Dr Allen in Cowfield, sent to the appropriate health department, resulted in the delivery of a magnificent blue tricycle.

I had hidden the machine behind the cottage, wanting to surprise Robby on his return from school.

'There's something round the back I want you to see, Robby,' I told him when we got home.

I followed behind him. The upper part of his body swayed from side to side and he was walking slowly. His arched body turned the corner of the cottage ahead of me and then I heard his shout of delight.

'Is this bike mine?' he shouted.

Judith had been watching from the kitchen, and she ran out of the house to join us.

'Of course it's yours, Robby,' I said, and the next moment I was helping him to mount the machine.

I ran alongside him as he pedalled up the long driveway. Within a few days he had mastered the technique of riding it in his own fashion. Suddenly he had the means of travelling faster by his own physical efforts. The effect on his morale was immediate. I was angry with myself for not thinking of the idea much earlier. Then one afternoon, he took the corner at the top of the safe driveway too fast. The tricycle toppled over and landed on top of Robby. Judith was out shopping and I ran up the drive to answer Robby's cries for help, my mind filled with dread. Had he broken a leg? What had the accident done to other parts of his body? I picked him up carefully and he was able to stand without assistance. But I carried him back to the cottage, laid him on the sofa and phoned Dr Allen, asking him to call as soon as possible. I could not see any serious damage, only cuts or bruises, but if Robby had suffered a fracture, it might be a big setback for him. Robby looked very white. I blamed myself now for getting the machine. Supposing he had to spend a long period in bed recovering? Any period of inactivity would be detrimental – a long one could be disastrous.

'I'm sorry, Dad,' he said, 'I was going too fast, wasn't I?'

Judith arrived at the same time as Dr Allen. Within minutes we were assured that to all outward appearances nothing serious had occurred. However, the doctor recommended that until some X-rays had been taken, Robby should not go to school. A few days later, X-rays showed no fractures and by the end of the week, Robby was riding his tricycle again. Judith began to question the wisdom of letting Robby have the machine, but he promised to go more slowly, and in the end, Judith agreed that the beneficial effect to Robby's muscles and morale far outweighed the possible dangers. We knew that Robby could not possibly compete with able-bodied children in many physical activities. To do so might heighten his feelings of inadequacy. But he wanted to try everything. It was shortly after this fall that he asked me about the chances of becoming a boarder at Hollingbury. Judith and I were temporarily in a quandary. The dilemma was increased by a visit from Judith's parents.

Ruth and Ralph were very happy to see that Robby was still walking and defying the prognosis. But they were still anxious for us to live in America, where they still considered that Robby would get better medical treatment. They were totally opposed to him becoming a boarder. But there was one very encouraging improvement in Robby's behaviour towards them. Instead of becoming passive in the presence of his grandmother, he confidently faced her challenges.

'Robby,' Ruth pleaded tearfully to him, 'an English boarding school is too Calvinistic for someone like you!'

'What do you mean, Gandhi?'

'Calvinistic – don't they teach you anything at your school? Calvin was a hard, puritanical man.'

'It's not like that at Hollingbury,' he answered defiantly.

'Perhaps not, but I expect the atmosphere is cold and austere,' she went on, I'm sure it's no place for such a sensitive young man as you are, my Robby!'

When they had left us, calm returned, and Robby became so insistent about boarding at Hollingbury, that I arranged a meeting with Ted and Maidie to discuss the idea. They accepted with alacrity, adding that the other boys would be delighted. I stressed the need for Robby to do exercises. Finally they said I could see him each evening and put him through his exercises in the dormitory. Robby was delighted to be accepted, but saddened by the thought that he could not take the menagerie with him, to which had now been added a tortoise.

Robby had now defied the prognosis for three years. He was walking, but no longer able to jogtrot. Climbing stairs at home became difficult, but he still continued to battle up them. The stairs at Hollingbury, which he had to climb to reach his dormitory, were not steep. He was able to get up them easily and they were spaced so widely apart that descending was just as safe and simple. He began his term as a boarder. Each evening I called at Hollingbury and put Robby through his paces. There were six other boys in his dormitory and they joined in the fun. It was a unique experience for the other boys, and it was not long before I was asked to smuggle into the dormitory all manner of items and foodstuffs. I was able to meet some of their less ambitious requests and I made sure that I was not contravening the rules of the school. Nonetheless, I was able to add certain items of food to the ones they managed to amass for illicit meals, after the lights had been turned out. It was a remarkable experience for me as well as for them. Robby seemed to enjoy Hollingbury even more.

Judith had meanwhile been saving up for a surprise winter sports holiday. We were all delighted, and at the end of term we took Robby and David to a small resort in the Italian Alps called Livigno. The package tour operator had been told about Robby's walking problem. We were informed that the coach journey from Milan to the Alps would take about five hours. In the event, it took twenty-four. Fog at Milan diverted our aircraft to Genoa. When we disembarked at Genoa we noticed a coach leaving the passenger's exit park. It was our coach, on the way to Milan to collect us. We discovered this about four hours later, when our guide had been pressed to tell us why there was no coach for our party. Eventually our coach returned from its useless journey and we set off for the Alps. Even so, Robby and David were delighted at the mix up. It added to their excitement of travel and, as it happened, resulted in our coach crossing the Alps as the sun was rising behind the mountains. It was a splendid greeting from nature, and Robby and David stared wide-eyed out of the coach windows. The snow reflected the sun's rays and threw them back to the mountain tops.

Although Robby could no longer risk being put on skis, I took him down the slopes on mine. We had snowball fights, sleigh rides and happiness all the time in Livigno. But it was to be the last time that Robby could stand on his feet in the snow.

As Robby's muscular strength weakened, there was a corresponding sense of urgency, sometimes bordering on over-enthusiasm, about his exercises. But the battle had to continue, there could be no giving up. Robby's response to the extra effort was incredibly brave. Lying on his back, he would attempt to swing his body forward to touch his toes. I would kneel beside him and as the top half of his body made its fruitless effort to rise, I would place my hands behind his back and push him gently forward. He refused to give up the fight of beating his lazy muscles.

There are over six hundred muscles in our bodies, and with every movement we make we use muscles. Robby had the six hundred plus, like all of us, but unlike us, instead of growing stronger as he grew up, they were growing weaker. Judith fought on with us and Robby continued to live and work with the able-bodied boys at Hollingbury. He frequently fell, but he got up as quickly as he could and kept up with the others. But although Judith and I knew that we had to win the war, we both knew that we were losing one of its battles. The falling increased, and blood on his knees and torn trousers became the marks of his courage.

Soon after he reached the age of thirteen, he could not get up without help, and this development terminated his spell as a boarder at Hollingbury. He had learnt to live with others, although he was probably unaware of any moral strengthening of his life. But we could see how much his character had improved. And self-discipline was to become an increasingly important quality in his life.

He was still able to ride his tricycle, though David or I had to run alongside it. It was becoming difficult for Robby to push the pedals down hard and this made his balance on the saddle precarious. I found an old pedal push car in a junk yard in

Brighton. So this became a safer way for Robby to propel himself quicker than he could walk. Then his feet began to slip on the pedals of the push car. He loved steering the machine, so I pushed or pulled him around the driveway. We fought on together, and when he was at school, he fought on his own. His walk was becoming heavy, his feet turned in more, which necessitated the wearing of special shoes.

Although it was a slow process, he could still dress himself and push his body into a sitting position in bed. On many occasions, Judith would watch and follow Robby as he struggled up the stairs, or battled to make his body move during exercises. She felt profoundly helpless and powerless. And once, when she had gone downstairs after saying goodnight to Robby, I heard her crying in the kitchen. She was at the sink washing dishes and I went to her, and put my arms around her. She did not react to my embrace. She did not seem to realise that I was there.

'What is it, darling?' I said.

'He is going, isn't he, Hugh?'

'It's a battle to keep him walking now – yes. You know that as well as I do.'

I looked at her and said to myself – when he cannot walk, what then? Would she still maintain that Robby did not have Duchenne dystrophy? It was no use crossing those bridges yet. She had stopped crying and was busy with the dishes again. Taking great care to be silent, I went out of the cottage for a walk up the drive towards the big house. The air was cool but I felt listless. I felt alone, and in the dark, words repeated themselves. 'He's going! He can't keep walking much longer.' Ted and Maidie were becoming concerned. 'He's just not able to keep up, Hugh. He's walking so slowly now.'

Robby did not once ask what was happening to his body. He seemed so intent on trying to be normal and making his muscles stronger that perhaps the thought never entered his head. 'I knew I had to keep walking, Dad,' he remembers now.

As I walked slowly back to the cottage that night, I knew something of great importance was going to happen soon. There would be no alternative. I was distinct about it in my mind. I had to have Robby prepared for it and Judith even more so. Sometime soon he was going to need a wheelchair. The doctor had warned me that when that moment arrived, Robby would be confined to it – forever.

Chapter Sixteen

Robby had defied the prognosis for three years, and there was a lifetime in three years. The old look back with nostalgia, but it is living now, in the present, that matters. Robby lived in the present, like his companions, and he had led a full physical life with other boys. I knew the faces of many of those boys well, though I could not remember all of the names. They had all consciously or unconsciously played their parts in helping Robby and perhaps helped themselves as a result. The staff and the boys at Hollingbury Court School had done more than most. Outside the cottage I said to myself aloud, 'He's going to go on living.' Nobody heard, and I said again, chiefly for my own benefit, 'He's going to go on living,' and when I got back inside the cottage I said to Judith, 'Whatever happens to Robby – if he gets so weak that he needs a wheelchair – we battle on, darling, don't we?' I felt my stomach go empty as I spoke the words.

She just looked at me.

'I'm going to have a chat with Ted tomorrow,' I went on, 'to see if we can find a way to make things easier for them and Robby.'

Slowly, uneasily, she turned her head away from me. 'Yes – and God give us strength,' Judith cried.

Then she was in my arms, and we both knew that another battle was only just beginning.

Ted was keen for Robby to stay on as a day boy at Hollingbury. He felt that whilst Robby remained so obviously happy at the school, it was out of the question to take him away from that environment. Robby wanted to stay, but he was worried about his lack of mobility. We could not let this continue. There were probably other boys who disliked school, yet they had to stay. Robby liked it, but might have to leave. Then the Fates suddenly dealt us a cruel blow, or so it seemed at the time.

We still played our game of football and cricket in a quiet corner of the driveway. There was the need for much 'make believe' to keep Robby's interest alive. We pretended that we each represented a famous team of eleven players and worked out a league table. For cricket, Robby would bat, and if his timing was right, he would manage to hit the ball. Runs were scored by the ball reaching a certain point – the edge of the grass five yards from the wicket scored two runs – if the ball rolled on the grass, it scored four. A full toss on to the grass scored six. He loved the involvement. But one afternoon we had just entered the cottage after a game of cricket when he tripped and fell. I lifted him to his feet, but he complained of a slight pain in his right ankle. I carried him to the sofa, calling out for Judith. We inspected the ankle carefully, but we could not see even the slightest of swellings. Dr Allen was called and he confirmed that there was nothing seriously wrong. He did not even suggest an X-ray this time. But the next morning when Robby tried to stand on his feet, he found that he could not keep his balance. I was holding him all the time so he did not fall over. I had helped him to sit up in bed, and watched as he slowly took off his pyjama jacket. He had put on his vest and shirt, prior to standing. I had to help him at this stage with his underpants. But on this morning, I knew that if I released my hold on his body, it would collapse like a pack of cards.

'What's wrong with my feet, Dad? They don't want to take any weight, do they?'

'No – let's put you back in bed a moment, shall we? I'll get Mum to come and help.'

'I'll be late for school!'

'I'll get you there in time – don't worry.'

But he did not go to school that day, and in the late afternoon a wheelchair was delivered for Robby.

Robby was upstairs in his room making a model car. Judith cried when she saw the chair.

'Judith, darling – it's going to be wonderful for him – look!' I said.

I opened the sides of the chair, sat down and began to wheel myself round the room.

'It's going to give back to Robby some of the mobility he has been losing – can't you see – it's going to make such a difference to him.'

But I was thinking myself how ugly the contraption looked. A wheelchair – a chair on wheels. Could not modern man produce a better product for disabled people? It looked cumbersome and uncomfortable.

'It will have to do, until they find a cure,' Judith said.

'You believe he has dystrophy?'

'Hugh, until they find a cure for his problem, or a miracle, or something, I only believe in one thing – that we never give up.'

One of the wheelchair's tyres was too soft and the small front guide wheels squeaked as they turned. I went into the kitchen to get an oil can and a tyre pump. When I got back with them, Judith was sitting in the wheelchair.

'You look like a little old lady,' I said, and smiled.

'I feel like one – it's horrible in this chair, it's horrible,' she repeated.

Simon, our labrador, was sniffing round the tyres. Mee and Oww appeared from the kitchen, Simon growled at them and they hurried away. I took Judith's hands in mine and gently pulled her out of the wheelchair. Her reaction to the chair was giving me strength.

'Who said, "we never give up"? Robby's got to go on feeling he's as independent as he possibly can be. The chair will give him a lot more mobility than he's had. It will be much better for him at Hollingbury.'

'It will?'

'Yes. They are quite happy to have him in a wheelchair. I've already spoken to Ted and Maidie about it.'

'What about the other boys?'

'What about them?'

'They might tease him and…'

'Darling! What is this chair going to mean to us? Is it a symbol of the beginning of the end? Of failure? Of giving in?'

'No, but how's Robby going to feel when he sees it?'

'We'll find that out right now!'

I went quickly up the stairs, and Simon decided to chase after me. I had mentally worked on this moment for a long time. How could a wheelchair be treated as a positive symbol? In Robby's case, the doctors felt it might be best to have a long preparatory talk with him. I had agreed, but 'the best laid schemes of mice and men, gang aft a-gley'. Simon loved jumping onto Robby's bed, but as we entered his bedroom, he changed his mind this time and jumped onto Robby's table. The model car fell to the floor, but before Robby could register surprise or anger, Simon began to lick his face. This made Robby laugh loudly, which in turn brought Judith up from downstairs. I could think of only one thing. Whilst Robby was laughing and Judith more relaxed – now was the moment. It is important to be ready when luck and timing coincide.

'Downstairs, Robby,' I said to him, 'there is something for you.'

He was still laughing. Simon had jumped to the floor and had one of Robby's slippers in his mouth. Judith pulled it away.

'So come on,' I said, and picked Robby up in my arms and carried him downstairs. Judith and Simon followed.

Robby was in my arms when he saw the chair. 'What's that doing?' he said. 'Is that for me?'

'Yes, Robby,' I said, 'and I'm going to put you in it, now.' The expression on his face was more puzzled than concerned – Judith stood watching from the door. I lowered him gently into the chair. I took hold of the arm rests and moved the chair slowly backwards and forwards. Robby's hands seemed to fall naturally on to the top of the wheels.

His hands remained on the steel rims as I continued to move the chair. He began to smile, and then he spoke.

'It's great, Dad. Let me move it myself.'

I moved away and went to Judith. I put my arms around her shoulders and we watched Robby push the wheels with his hands and arms. He turned the chair within its own circumference – he moved it quickly forward and then stopped it, suddenly. He propelled it backwards, then forwards. He laughed at his clumsy efforts to jerk the chair on to its back wheels. He was obviously delighted with his ease of movement. His arms were strong.

Robby spent the next few days handling his wheelchair at home, and by the time I took him to Hollingbury, he had become adept in its use. It almost seemed a relief for him to sit in the chair and yet move in any direction he chose. However, the big test was to come at school. David Robertson met me at the entrance, for he had agreed to keep a special eye on Robby. I lifted Robby from the car into the wheelchair. I had taken Simon with us and as I opened the car door, he had jumped out and caused a noisy distraction by running straight through to the main hall. Suddenly boys appeared from nowhere, and two of them grabbed Simon by his collar. They brought him out to me and I put him back in the car. The boys were looking at Robby, and one of them said, 'Hullo, what are you doing in that thing?'

Robby smiled and replied, 'I can move much faster now.'

'Can I have a go in it?' the other boy asked. 'Run along inside now,' said David.

'Oh sir! Can't we have a go?'

The look on David's face worked wonders on the two boys. They disappeared inside rapidly. David took Robby away from me into the school buildings. For the rest of that day Judith and I waited impatiently for the time to pass.

'Are they going to treat Robby as though he is an invalid?' Judith voiced one of her inner fears.

'Of course they won't,' I said, but I remembered when I was a boy at school. There were the 'odd' children – the ones who suffered from a physical affliction. The pigeontoed, the lispers, and once there had been a boy with a pronounced hunched back. Charles Laughton was the rage at that time. He swung from the bells of Notre Dame as the Hunchback, so the boy was called Charlie. Another had certain gorilla characteristics. He was called 'Jubilee', after a gorilla at that time residing in London's zoo.

One sees the typical misfits of a school, and like adults, boys can often be unkind to each other. But Robby's problems lay deeper. Sickness to some of us is to wake up with a headache and a sore throat. But we know the unpleasant symptoms will pass. If we stay in bed we know that we can get up and walk – run, when we are fit again.

Dr Stewart-Wallace and Dr Allen had stressed the importance of daily therapy, active, assisted active, not done beyond the point of fatigue. Robby could still manage a few paces at a time. These were to be encouraged, and during that first day in a wheelchair at Hollingbury, the staff promised to supervise Robby. If he felt like a spell out of the wheelchair they would help him. I told Judith about these arrangements, but we both remained worried and apprehensive.

Judith came with me to collect him that day, and we got to the school a little earlier than usual. As we went into the main hall, we saw Maidie at the far end. When she saw us, she hurried our way. As she got closer to us, I could see the very worried expression on her face. I took one of Judith's hands in mine and tried to give her a reassuring grip. I felt the tension in her body.

'Hullo you two,' Maidie said, 'let's go to Ted's study and have a chat.' And she smiled. On the way, she went on, 'He's had a great first day.'

Again the world seemed good, and inside the study we were given the news. The first news of other people's reactions to a boy in a wheelchair.

'It's been quite a day for him, and us. There was no shortage of volunteers to help push Robby in his chair!' Maidie laughed, and continued, 'In fact, it's been a very lively day! During the breaks other boys wanted to ride in the chair and they invented a game that Robby was able to play with them.'

We soon realised that Robby was being made to feel 'one of the boys'. He was a boy in a chair on wheels. He was encouraged to do as much as he was capable of doing, without help. In addition to the normal activities, there was an extra amount of fun. This was caused by many of the children wanting a ride in the chair.

'Some of those boys were maniacs.' Robby can recollect those days vividly. 'They set up a kind of race track near the playing field. They weren't satisfied with the turns and hairpin bends. They even put obstacles on the course. Sometimes I was the driver – the one that sat in the seat. Then others would take over and I would play the starter.'

'Your chair used to have a difficult time,' I said, 'I've no idea how it survived.'

'Not only the chair, but all of us. The so-called driver was quite helpless. He just sat there and was pushed. Funny thing though, wheelchairs are such top heavy things, yet it was never turned over – no one fell out, and no one was ever hurt.'

Perhaps self-discipline played its part in the care taken during those games – or luck. Whatever the reason they helped to settle Robby into his new mobility of life.

To many of us, a wheelchair can be a symbol of immobility of mind as well as matter. The strangers stared at Robby when I took him to Brighton for walks along the sea front.

'I don't really mind people staring at me – people, grown up people, stare at each other all day long.'

'But Robby,' I can say to him nowadays, 'you didn't like the stares of other children, did you?'

'No, Dad, you're right. They didn't stare at school. But I remember the ones I didn't know used to stare at me in the streets. People still do that, don't they? I feel better when people look at me naturally, the way they look at you.'

'I get the most extraordinary looks at times, Robby! So does your mother, when she is, all dressed up.'

When the wheelchair became a part of his life, it also became another limitation that Robby had to learn to live with. In that framework of survival there was no room for depression. The chair could become a breastplate behind which he could shelter. Or it could be the means of discovering a new movement of life. The success of such movement would depend mostly on other people. Helping Robby might make them better people. Robby could make a positive contribution to the lives of others. It takes the shadows as well as the light to make a beautiful painting.

Judith went through a period of deep pessimism about Robby's future. She did not show this in front of him, but at night when he was in bed she would become gloomy and despondent. She hated the way strangers looked at Robby in his wheelchair.

'Why can't they understand what it must be like to be pushed around all day,' she said one night, 'why can't they stop staring at him?'

'A lot of that problem may be in your mind. Darling, for God's sake, let's be positive.'

'For God's sake,' she repeated my words. 'What the hell does He care about Robby's fate?'

The local parson had called to see us once. He had too many cares of his own to worry much about ours. But he had to bear the burden of a disastrous marriage, which ended in separation and dark looks from his bishop. For tea he preferred whisky, which under his personal circumstances was understandable. But we seemed to give him more comfort and cheer than he gave to us. Michael Stephen once told us he had 'given the vicar up for Lent'. It was not easy to argue against Judith's lack of faith at that time, and in that place. I often wondered how much Robby was aware of what was happening to his body. It did not seem necessary or possible to discuss it with him. Of course he knew what was happening, but like the rest of the world, not how... or why. Robby battled on against his lazy muscles, his 'bloody' lazy muscles, as he often called them.

About this time he began to use some four-letter words with greater frequency than taste allowed. His school hours gave little opportunity for this type of swearing. A discreet and tactful enquiry at Hollingbury by myself provided proof that Robby was not using the expletives during the day. Judith and I discussed the problem and we suddenly hit upon the reason. Up to the time of the wheelchair, he had been able to let off steam. When David was staying with us, we would often have wrestling matches and Robby would join in. There would be fights with plastic washing up containers filled with water. But the wheelchair had changed the pattern of his life in terms of those games.

Many boys can let off steam on the games fields. Others, frustrated by living in towns, and lacking self-discipline, by fighting on the terraces of football stadiums. The need for boys to have outlets for excess physical energy is never under dispute. Boredom often leads to an excess of venom in the brain, and Robby was releasing this by using unacceptable swear words in our presence. We suddenly realised that physical exercise was not the only way to let off steam. There are mental ways of achieving this, and one of them is to swear. Another way is to argue, and once we had understood this, the answer was simple. It was at mealtimes that Robby was encouraged to let himself go, mentally. The conversation would be directed towards a controversial subject and at the appropriate moment I would make a disputatious comment. It was not difficult to get a reaction from Robby, and if David was also present they would both have a verbal battle with me. The dining table became a centre of discussion and argument. Although Robby sometimes used four-letter words to gain emphasis to his views and ideas, he gradually stopped using them. I used the same words back at him, and the first time I did so, it took him by surprise. It was not long before he realised that the swear words added little to his arguments. They became vicious and pointless words aimed at nothing. We also laughed a lot at those mealtimes – they had good entertainment value.

But the frustrations of confinement to a wheelchair became a very real problem. He still slept upstairs, and now I had to carry him up and down. There was no room on the ground floor for a bedroom and we worried about the psychological effect of this lack of self-help. As his muscles weakened there was a corresponding increase in his weight. He was not getting fatter, like so many Duchenne dystrophy boys – he was getting thinner. But in my arms he became a dead weight to carry. He was very conscious of this extra burden on other people. He would apologise for the inconvenience he caused. It became important for him to avoid being complicated about the problem.

'Robby,' I said to him one evening, 'you know how much we love you, don't you?'

'Yes, Dad.'

'When love is strong there's nothing it can't do for people. When we carry you from your chair to your room, or pull it up steps, or take you to the cinema – whatever we do is done because we love you. There's no need to be over apologetic to people.'

'No? Well, I can see what you mean about us at home. But what about people who don't love me?'

'That's what's known as a very good question,' I smiled at him. 'By all means thank people who help you – but don't get complicated about it.'

'OK I won't, Dad.'

He had highlighted the help a family can give when that unit is motivated by love. As the front door of a house, a flat or any home opens, sometimes the warm aura of love floats into our veins. It cannot be seen, but it can be felt – inside ourselves. We tried to make our family a positive, loving unit and yet not allow any of its members to suffer unduly for the sake of a disabled child. We were all individuals with the right to exist as such. It really meant everyone pulling together, including Robby. This became more and more apparent as the relationship grew between David and Robby.

Some years earlier, we had bought David a guitar in Haverfordwest. As the years passed he played the instrument with increasing skill, and one day, soon after Robby was confined to the wheelchair, David taught him some chords to play. Robby's fingers were strong and he quickly demonstrated the musical talent he possessed. But Judith began to feel the strains of living with a son in a wheelchair. 'I still refuse to believe he has Duchenne dystrophy,' she said to me, 'but if he has, then what?'

I reached out and touched her cheek. It was the first time she admitted the possibility.

'I'll try and keep you strong,' I said.

'Yes, I know you will.'

Strength alone was not enough, for one day, when Robby was playing his guitar with David, she suddenly burst into tears and ran out of the living room. The boys stopped playing.

'What's wrong with Judith?' David asked.

'I'll find out. That's a good duet you're both playing. Go on playing it.' I left them to search for Judith.

She had gone to our bedroom. She had thrown herself on the bed and was quietly crying into a pillow. We could hear the guitars strumming below.

'Judith, darling – you've got to fight with us. If you can't cope, nor can I.'

'I know, I'm sorry Hugh. I'm pretty strong most of the time, thanks to you, but watching David and Robby, I suddenly thought that one day Robby's fingers may be too weak to play the guitar! Have you thought of that?'

'Yes. So what?'

'So what! Is that all you can say?'

'What do you think he'll do then? Nothing?'

'You know what I mean,' she said.

I was beginning to feel physically as well as mentally tired in the evenings now. As in most families, there never seemed to be enough money. There might have been so many more things we could have done for Robby, if only we had had more spare cash. Judith's parents sent some dollars from time to time. They still wanted us to live in the States permanently, so they were not anxious to over help. In any case, they were now getting old and needed all their money to survive in America.

'Yes. I know what you mean. But Robby has got to live a full life, and we all have each other. Things could be worse. Pray to God that his fingers don't get weak, but that doesn't mean that he shouldn't play the guitar whilst he can does it?'

'But when he can't, what then?'

'He'll do something else.'

'Such as?'

'Oh! God, Judith! I don't know! Some people paint with their toes!'

That made her look at me. For a moment we stared at each other, and then we laughed.

We never did quarrel for long. It takes a long time for a good quarrel to grow in Judith or myself. That, and our sense of humour were qualities in our favour. They were important qualities in Robby and David. Whenever possible, we did everything together, trying to overcome barriers with laughter. Some of these barriers were associated directly with the wheelchair.

It became very difficult to get Robby onto the lavatory until Dr Allen suggested we try a mobile toilet frame. This was a lavatory seat, fixed to a frame, which in turn had wheels at each corner. Robby would be placed on the seat and then pushed over the lavatory pan. He was not very happy with this arrangement, for although it was quite comfortable, it was a production getting him organised. Then one day, David named the contraption 'The Crap Mobeel', and ever after, Robby enjoyed the journey whenever nature called. Even so, the dangers of falling still applied when he was sitting. The able-bodied assume that a sitting position is safe. But it can be extremely dangerous for the Duchenne dystrophic boy. Many have fallen forward from a sitting position and suffered fractures. One morning, whilst Robby was on his 'Mobeel' I left him for a moment to answer the telephone. Judith was downstairs getting breakfast, and as the telephone was in our bedroom it was quicker for me to take the call. I had only been on the phone for a few seconds when I heard the noise. I threw the telephone to the floor and ran to answer Robby's screams.

He was lying face down on the floor. He could not fully straighten his legs because of the muscles' contractures. He looked so helpless. As I lifted him gently, blood was gushing out of his mouth. The shock of the fall was making him tremble. By the time I laid him on his bed, Judith had arrived. Recently, I reminded him about that terrible morning.

'I don't know how it happened,' he said. 'I remember trying to move forward a bit on the seat. The next moment I crashed to the floor.'

'We were going through the drama as much as you were.' 'Nonsense, Dad,' Robby smiled, 'I was the one who lost two front teeth!'

Two front teeth. At the time it seemed like the end of our world, for the flowing blood hid the gap caused by his loss of the teeth. When he stopped crying and was calmer, we could see the reason for so much blood. Judith had called Dr Allen, and that morning I took Robby to the dentist in Horsham. Within a few days Robby had a denture with two teeth.

'Hasn't he enough to put up with,' Judith had said, 'without that happening?'

'Yes,' I said, 'but it was my fault. I shouldn't have left him alone on that seat.'

'You can't blame yourself,' she said.

There has to be a first time, but it taught me to be ready in future for any first time. There is no excuse for lack of vigilance, even if there are reasons. Knowing what can happen is the best preventative.

Chapter Seventeen

As various aids became necessary for Robby, we treated them as aids to help himself. There was no giving in to passivity. We began to discover how many aids and helpful organisations there are in Britain. However, the fight to survive and overcome every hurdle has to come from within the family unit. That means knowing the supreme importance of love and understanding. There was also a third necessity in our life... money.

The doctors were always helpful, but there was no 'Hope' for Robby. We met some families whose problems were similar to ours, but Judith found this involvement distressing at times. We learnt of fathers who did not help, and most families passively accepted the prognosis. We needed strength to keep Robby moving, to keep trying and hoping. We also needed another type of home for Robby. A bungalow, with accommodation on one floor seemed to be an ideal choice. But for that, we needed more money, as bungalow-type property in Sussex is always in high demand. We began to plan starting a small business which we hoped might provide the money for Robby's needs. Then, when our plans were about to materialise, problems at Hollingbury Court School started upsetting Robby.

Twice a week I took him to Crawley where he was able to swim in a specially heated pool. This hydrotherapy was of tremendous help, for in the water he was able to exercise muscles without any risk of over-strain. He still did early morning exercises with me before school, but it was now difficult to arouse his enthusiasm for them. He needed help with all his lavatory functions. The staff at school coped with this problem, but the extra fuss involved made Robby feel 'different'. Fun with the wheelchair had been replaced by an indifference to it, in terms of the other children. They tended to ignore him, though this was in no way the fault of the staff. They just were not able to *give* him the attention he needed. The physical care of Robby was becoming more and more a major aspect of his daily routine. Then a visit to a physiotherapist resulted in Robby becoming *very* passive.

'Let her do it,' he said, referring to the therapist at Crawley. 'There's nothing I can do about my lazy muscles myself now.'

'But there is, Robby!' I said. 'If you want to take the easy way in life, the rewards might be correspondingly less. *You've* got to fight, Robby – more than *ever* before.'

'What's the point?' he asked.

'So that when a cure is found for your problem, your body will be in the best possible condition to benefit from the cure.'

I stressed the need for. him to do exercises himself and threw myself into encouraging him I did exercises with him, including those he was able to perform in the wheelchair. All the time, Judith watched the slow deterioration of her son.

One afternoon, on the way home from school, Robby said, 'What exactly is wrong with me, Dad?'

How could I reply? By telling him he had Duchenne dystrophy? I had already decided the time was not right. Dr Allen supported me in that decision, for he felt that in Robby's case it might lead to apathy. He might read somewhere that the Duchenne boy's muscles finally cease to work – meaning that everything has to be done for him. He has to be fed, he has to be dressed. The last muscles to go are the breathing muscles. The Duchenne boy catches a cold – the muscles are not strong enough to clear his throat. So he stops breathing.

'There's this terrible weakness in your muscle fibres, Robby. Your muscles are made up of a lot of fibres – those are the parts that lengthen and shorten.'

'I see,' he said. 'And I must go on trying to make them do as much work as possible.'

It was clearer to Robby now, but for Judith it was too clear. One day she cried out to me, 'I want to kill him! I want to put him out of his misery!'

'How miserable is he?' I said. 'How much do we know? What is going on in his mind? Darling – you're miserable right now – shall I kill you?'

She spoke slowly, making each word count.

'He has to be pushed from classroom to classroom. When the other boys go out to play, he can only watch. When…'

'When he plays the guitar,' I cut in, 'he's so happy. When he plays games with us – when he feels the physical efforts he makes are helping him, his eyes light up.'

'And we have to watch him fight and struggle just to turn over in bed.'

'You couldn't kill him, without killing yourself and me… and David.'

About this time Ted and Maidie said they wanted to see us. I knew before we met them that Robby's time at Hollingbury was drawing to a close. From the talks I had with him, I could tell that Robby had lost interest in the school. It now presented too many stresses and frustrations for a severely disabled child. Hurstpierpoint would have the same problems for him to an even greater degree. Normal, ordinary schools, were becoming out of the question for Robby. They were neither adapted nor geared to his special needs. Ted and Maidie both felt that unless a state school could cope, then the only fair alternative for Robby would be a 'special' school. Hollingbury had done so much for Robby – we would never forget the magnificent help it had given. We became even more aware of that help as we searched for another school. Even where the teaching staff were confident of coping, Robby was adamant about the practical difficulties he had already experienced at Hollingbury.

'If I want to go to the loo,' he said, 'it's always such a bloody production. I can't even do up the zip of my trousers at times! Someone else has to do that for me, don't they?'

'But they will always help you, Robby.'

'That's not the point, Dad. How would you like it? Having to be helped every time you want to spend a penny?'

'There will always be people around happy to do that for you. Just like Hollingbury.'

'There were no girls at Hollingbury. That school in Horsham is full of them!'

The everyday actions that the able-bodied take for granted are often impossibilities for the Duchenne boy. He needs help. But he must get that help with the minimum of fuss or embarrassment. He wants above all to be treated as a normal human being. The friends we had were full of conflicting advice. One suggested that we send him to his grandparents in New York. Another suggested that he remain at home with a tutor. An old friend of mine thought it would be best for Robby to be put in an institution.

'Better for him – or us?' I said.

'For all of you. Can't you see how much better? He would have all the aids he needs. There would be doctors on hand. You and Judith could lead much fuller lives.'

He was obviously concerned about the welfare of us all – he was close to some of our problems. But after he had gone Judith and I talked late into the night. There was only one thought in our mind – what was best for Robby? We knew that an institution, no matter how well run, would take our love out of his life. That weekend, David came to stay with us. He brought us good fortune. On the first morning of his holiday, the education department of the West Sussex County Council phoned. Mr Maxted, an official of the council, arranged to call on us a few days later. It was this kind man who first told us of the existence of a boarding school called the Lord Mayor Treloar College.

Chapter Eighteen

The school was founded in 1908 as the result of an appeal made by Sir William Treloar during his term of office as Lord Mayor of London. The aim of the school remains the same – to make boys and girls able to compete with life however severe their disabilities. It sounded an ideal place for Robby, and when I spoke to him about the school he was not unenthusiastic. To be 'not unenthusiastic' was perhaps the nearest we could get to enthusiasm. Mr Maxted thought that Robby might like the atmosphere and setting of the school. There was only one way to find out and we arranged a visit to Treloar College.

A week before this visit we received a letter from Judith's mother in which she recommended that we take Robby to see Dr John Wilson, a consultant neurologist at Great Ormond Street Hospital. This doctor was to play an important part in the momentous decisions that lay ahead for us. Our continued ambition for Robby was to bring interest back to his life – in fact, to make his life full of interest in spite of the wheelchair and the prognosis.

Dr Wilson seemed very pleased with Robby's physical condition. He thought that Robby was less severely affected than many of the children he knew of the same age. He added that this was probably due to the quality of his care. This gave us all a much-needed morale boost. He told me that some parents of Duchenne boys have a tendency to surrender to the prognosis. He told me never to give up hope and always make Robby feel that he had something to live for, to fight for – to make him feel wanted, to let him mix with other children and feel part of a group. Man's reach should always be beyond his grasp. The more spurs Robby had, the better. We took this wise and timely advice with us to Lord Mayor Treloar College.

David came with us, and as we saw the school for the first time he said to Robby, 'Here you are entering prison – just like Hurstpierpoint!'

This was not the most helpful of remarks. However, as the afternoon passed I could sense that Robby was becoming more impressed with the school. It is centred on an Elizabethan mansion, but the classrooms and accommodation are purpose-built to meet the needs of the disabled child. It has its own gymnasium and heated indoor swimming pool. There is an impressive assembly hall, art and craft departments, music rooms, library and a modern medical centre. Everything was accessible to the wheelchair, and Robby felt this ease and naturalness of movement. The staff we met seemed kind and understanding. Robby would be able to work for the CSE examination or the GCE 'O' Level.

Robby recalled that first impression a few years later. 'It certainly seemed an OK place to me. I enjoyed my boarding time at Hollingbury and thought it would be like that.'

The school is situated in attractive and spacious surroundings near Alton, Hampshire, but it is residential only. Robby would have to be a boarder. There are boarding and day schools for normal boys. Here was a boarding school for disabled boys. Should he go as a boarder, and would he benefit from the experience? We called in the help and advice of Dr Wilson. He wrote to us, saying that a number of his patients attended the school. They were not isolated from the mainstream of normal activity as they would be in a normal school. Everything was adapted for the disabled child. He thought that faced with a similar problem, he would send his own child to the school. He added that it would be with a very great sadness, knowing the separation it would entail, but Robby would come home for all the normal school holidays, and would continue his schooling in a positive and disciplined atmosphere, with other children, where his intellect would have a good chance to develop.

Robby agreed to give it a try. The West Sussex Council undertook to pay the fees. Although there was a very great sadness for us as we drove away from Treloar on his first day, it was the same experience for most parents whose children are spending their first term as a boarder in a new school. We had tea with Robby's housemaster and his wife. Judith put on a brave face.

'I remember,' Robby said, 'I semi-enjoyed it at tea. But there was the thought of the days to come and being away from you all.'

A few weeks later I was back at Treloar once more, to collect Robby for his first leave weekend. We had exchanged some good letters and he seemed to have settled down quickly. I had spoken to his housemaster once or twice on the telephone and he confirmed that Robby was in good shape. This made me all the more worried and surprised when I first had a glimpse of his face. There was a large black circle around his left eye. But he was smiling.

'What on earth's happened to your eye, Robby?'

He looked around carefully and then said, 'Another boy hit it.'

'Oh did he!' I said. 'I would like to meet that boy right now and…'

'Please, Dad! I'm fine. I'm all right.'

'With that eye! It was a most cowardly thing for anyone to do – to hit you when you're in a wheelchair.'

'So was the boy who hit me!'

'You mean he was in a wheelchair, too?'

'Yes. He got me first.'

I took Robby across to our car, put him in the back seat, folded the wheelchair and almost threw it into the boot of the car. I left him sitting in the car and hurried away to find the housemaster.

On the way to his flat I passed some of the other students. They were like other boys from public, grammar or secondary modern schools. Some looked serious, some sad, others were laughing and talking. But there was the 'difference' from the others. Some were in wheelchairs, some walked without any sign of disablement, some had limbs missing. I saw Robby's housemaster, Mr Green, approaching. He waved and quickly came over to me.

'I was hoping to catch you before you saw Robby – would you come along to my flat?'

'Of course. I was trying to find you.'

He was a slightly built man in his early forties. I wondered how he managed to lift some of his pupils, but I was to learn from Robby that there was a wiry toughness behind his lightweight body. As soon as we reached the privacy of his flat, he began to apologise for Robby's eye.

'I don't know what started the fight, but I've severely reprimanded the other boy.'

'When did it happen?' I asked.

'Last night in the dormitory. I'm afraid it was probably something to do with the weekend leave spirit.'

I had every intention of creating a big fuss and demanding an inquiry into the matter. I said nothing.

'The doctor had a good inspection of Robby's eye,' Mr Green continued, 'there's no serious damage.'

'I thought Robby was settling down well,' I said.

'Oh, but he is! There are a few problems.'

'Such as?'

'Well, I'm sure you'll understand me when I say that Robby's accent is a bit upstage compared with some of the others. We have lots of boys from less privileged backgrounds.'

'Mr Green,' I said, 'I don't think we are exactly privileged people. However, I take your point about his accent. He's been teased a lot, has he?'

'Yes. But I'm sure it will pass.'

Robby had said nothing of this in his letters. We had moved to a bungalow near Horsham and it only took an hour to drive home. But it seemed like a hundred hours, for Robby talked about Treloar all the way. He hated the school – he found the work too difficult and he had no intention of 'trying' at all. The other boys did not like him and he certainly did not like them. I could only think of the disastrous weekend that lay ahead – and the deep disappointment for us all. As we got closer to home, I asked him why he had not written to me about the problems.

'I didn't want to disappoint you, Dad,' he said, 'I've really tried very hard to like it – it's no good. I've had enough of it.'

Judith managed to hide her true feelings until Robby had gone to bed. I was subjected to some harsh criticism from her, but the more she became determined to keep Robby at home, the more I began to think that perhaps Robby was 'putting it on' to a certain extent.

'You call that black eye putting it on!' she said. 'My poor boy – he's not going back! I feel afraid for him. Something terrible will happen.'

'Nothing terrible will happen to him.'

'But his eye!'

'That happens at normal schools.'

'But Robby isn't normal!' As soon as she had spoken those words she suddenly remained silent. We looked at each other.

'Isn't that the whole point,' I said. 'Isn't that what we've been fighting for all these years. Would you go to him now and say – Robby, you're not normal.'

'He knows that without us telling him.'

The next day Dr Allen came to inspect the eye. He sympathised and agreed that Robby's start at Treloar was inauspicious. However, he felt that it was only fair on the school and Robby to give it more of a chance. He even managed to persuade Judith to relent and not condemn so quickly. We needed time to think, and a weekend was not enough. I telephoned Mr Green and got permission for Robby to stay home for a few extra days. During that time there was an interesting development. On the morning of the first extra day Robby said that he was bored. He wanted to go to Brighton, but he soon realised that this was impossible. Judith and I had started the small business. She was able to cope on her own when I had to be at home with Robby during his holidays, for she was now unable to lift him herself, but she had to take the car to work with her. Then Robby insisted that he should be taken to the cinema in Horsham, but this was again impossible for the same reasons. By midday he said he wanted to talk to me about Treloar. He said that it was not so bad there really – but he did not like being bullied.

'How bullied are you?' I asked him. 'They get on at me. They don't like me.'

'You haven't gone back to wanting your own way all the time, have you Robby?'

'Well…' he hesitated, 'maybe – I don't know.'

We talked, and by the time Judith returned that evening, Robby was changing his mind about going back to Treloar. He had spent part of the day playing his guitar and reading. I had done some wheelchair exercises with him and taken him for a long walk in the afternoon.

We did not want him to feel that he was being pressurised into returning to Treloar. Judith had very reluctantly agreed that if Robby wanted to go back, then he could – provided no one bullied him. I instinctively thought that for his own sake, for his self-respect, he should try again. He was learning to fight a battle that was not peculiar to him. It was the one we all have to fight with greater or lesser degrees of success – that of facing life and not running away from it.

David came home from Hurstpierpoint for the evening and helped in the discussions. It became a family conference. The two boys were on each other's side and they both wanted to stay at home! I asked David in front of Robby if there was bullying at his school.

'Yes, but not nearly as much as there used to be,' he told us. 'In fact, it rarely occurs now… but if Robby has been bullied, then I sympathise with him. It's horrible.'

'There you are, Dad,' Robby agreed, 'you see?'

'Of course I see,' I said, 'I went through the same experiences.'

'It's a form of perversion,' said David. He was beginning to read much more.

'But don't you both agree that we should all try and finish things that we begin?' I suggested.

Finally, as David had to return to Hurstpierpoint, the conference came to an end. But the next morning, Robby said he would go back as long as the problems could be resolved. I telephoned Mr Green, and later that day Robby was once more installed as a boarder at Treloar. It proved to be the right decision.

At that time, normal schools were starting to take in less severely disabled boys. This meant that Treloar was taking much more seriously disabled boys than in the past. Although this led to additional problems and requirements, the staff were as dedicated as ever. They were full of care and devotion and, perhaps as important, they were trained to treat the boys as normal human beings. Therefore, discipline was part of that training. As soon as the problem of teasing had been sorted out, Robby began to make friends. His accent changed in proportion to his 'oral' surroundings. It was a fascinating experience, for within a term, he was dropping h's with abandon. That did not matter, though we encouraged him not to be too lazy in his speech when he was at home.

Treloar encouraged Robby to fight on and there was always a spur for Robby. The school ran on exactly the same lines as a normal boarding school. There was the same vexation at rules which forbade smoking or drinking for the younger students. But pointless privilege was on the way out for the older ones. In spite of the disablement problem, there were prefects who had authority over younger boys. Certain practices common to public schools were being re-examined and some old traditions were modified. Robby's bullying episode had highlighted that aspect of community life. Positive steps were taken to prevent its recurrence. Teamwork was of little account in terms of the playing fields, but it played a large part in everyday routine. The boys who could walk helped those in wheelchairs, by pushing them from classroom to classroom.

'That was one of the great things about Treloar, Dad,' Robby remembers, 'there were so many different types of disablement. We were all in the same boat, and yet different.'

There was a very wide range of physical disabilities, but each student was encouraged to be as independent as possible. Although many of the handicaps did not have a terminal prognosis, there were nonetheless many severe forms of disablement – polio, thalidomides, cerebral palsy, spina bifida, Robby's muscular dystrophy types, heart conditions, and the ones who could walk, the haemophiliacs. They were all adolescent human beings with brains and hearts, some good, some bad. Every day Robby worked and played with others who looked worse off than himself. Under these conditions he became kinder, more helpful, more willing to try to do his best. There were school plays and end-of-term concerts, music and work. The routine of work, of physically having to go to the classrooms, and be at meals on time, consolidated the self-discipline already taught at Hollingbury. The timetable had to be obeyed as much as it is in a normal school. This all strengthened Robby's resolve to fight his problems. Learning, passing examinations and failing some, made him interested in activities outside himself. But the most important breakthrough in terms of Robby developing a very keen interest in an activity outside himself was about to occur. Paradoxically, this was not an involvement of a sedentary nature – it was totally active.

Chapter Nineteen

One holiday, I took him to see Brighton and Hove Albion play football. That team and its affairs, its successes and its failures, have played an incalculable part in making Robby want to live, want to survive. But the first visit was not lightly undertaken. Judith and I talked it over for many weeks. Supposing Robby reacted with envy at so much physical activity going on around him? If the experience made him feel inadequate then it would have been wiser for him to stay away from football grounds. There was also the danger of becoming involved in a bottle-throwing accident from the terraces. It was worrying to think that it might be dangerous for a disabled person to watch a match because of the violence of football fans.

I stood behind his wheelchair at the ground with the barrier between us, and I was unable to see his face during the first half. It was no longer possible for him to turn his head round, so I could only catch occasional glimpses of his face, and then only a side view. He seemed to be enjoying himself. At half time, I went round to the front of the barrier. From the expression on his face it was obvious that our fears were groundless. His eyes were bright and shining with excitement.

'It's great, Dad, isn't it?'
'Yes. You're enjoying it very much?'
'What do you think, Dad! Say, can I have a cigarette?'
'You don't smoke, Robby!' I said with surprise.
'No. But you do, and I'm sure it'll calm my nerves.'
'No, Robby. I'm drawing the line there – no smoking.'

As his chest muscles weakened he was going to have enough problems breathing, without adding to them by inhaling tobacco.

'But Dad!'
'But no!'

At the end of the game I bought an Albion scarf and other supporter's paraphernalia. It was about this time that Brian Clough had his short reign as manager of the club.

He brought with him his usual enthusiastic approach to the game. This added greatly to Robby's sudden devotion to the team and to football. We had found a way of taking him outside himself even more.

I discovered a way of playing football with him in his wheelchair. I would roll the ball towards his feet and he would kick it between my open legs to score a goal. He would wear his Albion scarf and give a commentary on the game. He began to learn the history of the Brighton club, and took a keen interest in football in general. As the years passed he was to become deeply involved with the game.

His happy letters home from Treloar reflected his changed attitude towards the school. But physically his condition continued to deteriorate. As the strength of his arms weakened it became very difficult for him to propel his wheelchair. The only answer at Treloar was an electric wheelchair, but when he came home the self-propelled one was used. In this way he was able to have the use of both types.

'I found that although the electric chair got me from place to place easily, it also made me a bit lazier,' Robby commented recently. 'Lazier, in terms of doing exercises.'

Many of those exercises were now assisted. But the battle continued to keep his muscles moving from his own efforts. We were determined to prevent atrophy caused by disuse. I helped to stretch the contractures by slowly and steadily extending them to the point of pain. I interchanged ideas with the doctor at Treloar. Robby knew that there was always 'something being done' for him. Judith faced the problems with courage, but she found that visits to Treloar were full of deep emotion for her. This was not only because of Robby's disablement, but also from the sight of others whose bodies were badly deformed. This applied in particular to the thalidomide victims.

Then one day after seeing an end-of-term performance of *Toad of Toad Hall,* Judith's attitude changed. The boy playing Toad was very severely disabled. His head was large, his body short. He looked the part of a Toad. The boy was given a tremendous ovation for his performance. He looked so happy. Judith and I were introduced to the boy's parents, who were sharing the stage success of their son by hugging and congratulating him. They were very proud of him. The natural atmosphere made Judith forget her feelings of pity and self-consciousness, and from that moment those feeling never returned.

For many, there is the understandable sense of wanting to withdraw from surroundings of severe disablement. But if those people could participate, they would not feel so self-conscious. Perhaps they are frightened or nervous. Both these negative emotions can be harmful to the person experiencing them. The disabled person will have already suffered from the alien vibrations.

Just when the immediate period ahead again looked more settled for Robby, some setbacks occurred. Physically, he was holding his own. He watched television more, but he also listened to the radio, which helped to stretch his imagination. He became more involved with football and his team. In the summer months he began to take a greater interest in cricket. This occurred after I had taken him to see Sussex play at their ground in Hove. He liked a glass of beer, and one day he confided to me that he had the 'odd' cigarette at Treloar. He was trying to live more and more like the others, the able-bodied.

After his first term at Treloar, I had told him that he had muscular dystrophy. The moment had been right, for he had discussed the nature of the disease with me quite openly and without fear. It made us both more determined to fight those lazy muscles. He did not know about the terminal nature of Duchenne, but he did know that his muscles might get progressively weaker. I constantly urged him to continue the fight. We had no intention of giving up – we were all determined to win. The physical worsening of his body made us all the more resolute to fight the prognosis. Even now, when he was fifteen and his spine was more curved, we did exercises together. This gave him great encouragement. It was also of physical benefit, for he was able to sit for long periods without discomfort.

'Come on, Robby,' I would say to him, 'we're going to beat this, aren't we?'

Often he would agree, sometimes he felt the efforts were pointless.

'I'm getting weaker, Dad,' he would say, 'it's no use.'

'I'm not giving up, Robby! So you might just as well string along with me.'

I induced, encouraged and occasionally drove him into positive thought and action. But there were moments when I lost heart. There were certain chords on the guitar that he found difficult to play. His fingers no longer had the necessary length of reach and he could not exert enough pressure on the strings. Then we bought a second-hand drum set and the three of us played together. Judith sang and used her singing talent to great effect. The feeling of depression would pass.

Then one night, as I tucked him up in bed, he said he wanted to talk to me. At the end of the day, in the comfort and security of his bed, he would often tell me his innermost thoughts. I sat on the edge of his bed.

He said, 'There's no cure for my type of dystrophy. Is that true, Dad?'

'As yet there's no cure for any of the different types. But one will be found.'

'When, I wonder, when?'

'Maybe tomorrow, maybe your lazy muscles…'

'Oh God, Dad! I'm not a kid any longer! Don't call my muscles lazy! I've got this disease – I heard that I will die when I'm twenty!'

'Where did you hear that?'

'At Treloar – I read about it.'

'What did you read?'

'It said that you don't survive after your teens.'

'You're going to, Robby.'

'Come off it, Dad!'

'You're going to fight and prove them wrong.'

'We can't win Dad – I was talking to one of the boys at Treloar. He said there's no hope.'

'What the hell have we been doing all these years, then?'

'Wasting our time.'

'Thank you, Robby! Thank you for nothing.'

'I tell you – we might just as well give up.'

'If you think we're going to give up now, you're very mistaken.'

'Dad – they don't even know what causes it – how the hell can they find a cure then?'

'That's their problem, Robby. Ours is to battle on. Of course, if you want to become a plum pudding and sit around all day doing nothing.'

It became increasingly difficult to fight these moods of depression. Judith began to lose heart and even David lost stomach for the fight. He said that no matter how much he helped Robby to do exercises, the effect was the same.

'He seems to be getting weaker, Dad,' David said, 'soon, he's not going to have enough strength to hold his guitar.'

Judith suggested that if only we had a swimming pool in the garden, Robby could use it in the summer. But we could not possibly afford one, could we?

'What a marvellous idea,' I said. 'There must be some way to raise the money.'

'It would have to be heated for him too,' she said. We looked deeply into each other's eyes.

'You've got that "If you want something badly enough, you can get it" look in your eyes, darling,' I smiled at her.

'So have you,' she smiled back.

The building of the pool was quickly completed, and for a while it took us all outside ourselves. Robby swam with David every day during the summer holidays, and his muscles benefited by the ease of his movements in the water. But as the summer came to an end, the struggle began to repay the extra mortgage, and there were much higher electricity bills caused by the need for heated water. Then one day, Mee disappeared, never to return. Soon afterwards, Oww was killed by a car in the road in front of our bungalow.

Simon had now grown into a handsome dog, and Robby was able to gain extra comfort from the intelligent animal. But the fate of our cats was a tragedy, for we were all very close to them. Events seemed to be moving against us as they do from time to time in everyone's life. Robby even lost faith in his prayers, saying that God had no intention of answering his, so what was the point of prayer. But when the bottom of the hill has been reached, the climb up can start again.

Chapter Twenty

In all ages, in every civilisation, and all over the world, there have been divine healers, seers, soothsayers and cranks of many shapes and descriptions. People who have lost hope and confidence often go to the cranks. In the case of terminal illness, many feel that there is nothing to be lost in giving anything a try. Robby's faith in prayer was at its lowest ebb, and he needed a great boost for his morale.

It came suddenly, out of the blue, from acupuncture.

Aldous Huxley had once written, 'that a needle stuck in one's foot should improve the functioning of one's liver is obviously incredible. But as a matter of empirical fact, it does happen.' We were fortunate enough to be introduced to an acupuncturist who is not a crank – Dr J. D. Van Buren. This interesting and remarkable man was honest in his assessment of Robby's problem.

'You know that the prognosis is not good,' he said, 'and of course we do tend to get patients for whom orthodox medicine can do nothing to help. But let us see if we can do something for Robby.'

Later, Robby was having the needles painlessly inserted in various parts of his body. This was a remarkable reaction in terms of his previous fear of the hypodermic needle used in the blood tests. He looked relaxed and even asked Dr Van Buren what he was doing.

'Your body has been thrown out of balance with nature,' he told him. 'I'm trying to restore that balance so that you might lead a healthier life.'

'Are you going to get me to walk again?' Robby asked.

'I don't know Robby – but I'm going to have a damn good try.'

The effect of this positive remark on Robby was immediate. Suddenly there was someone in his life outside the family who might be able to help him. He smiled and waited for the treatment to finish. I took him out to the car and then went back to Van Buren.

'What do you really think?' I said.

'Whatever you want to think,' he smiled. 'I will do all I can to help Robby. His body's reaction to the therapy has been good. There is warmth in his legs now – and warmth is life.'

Since he had been in a wheelchair, his legs had been icy cold.

Every two weeks I took Robby to Van Buren. The doctor lived in Gerrards Cross, and during term time I collected Robby from Treloar and took him on that long journey for the acupuncture treatment. It was giving Robby hope, the quality that was lacking in other therapies. He said he always felt more relaxed after the treatment, and more than once remarked that his legs seemed stronger. When we first started the treatment, I was more sceptical about its benefits than Judith. Then as time passed and Robby's deterioration stopped, I began to feel confident about the possibilities. If Robby was going through a remission period, it was certainly becoming a long one.

During one of Robby's periodic examinations at Great Ormond Street, Dr Wilson said how pleased he was with Robby's physical condition. He was even more impressed with Robby's attitude and psychological improvement. He asked him if he liked Treloar.

'It's OK,' Robby replied, 'but has Dad told you about the acupuncturist?'

'No. Tell me more.'

'Well, he sticks needles in me and I feel better.'

'That's interesting,' Dr Wilson said. 'Anything that helps you feel better is fine.'

Robby was building up reserves of strength and courage.

One holiday Judith said to him that miracles can happen. David and Robby were quick to argue against such supernatural events. But a few days later they were more surprised than either Judith or myself when a Catholic teacher from a nearby school knocked on our door.

'Mr Franks,' his strong Irish accent echoed around the hall, 'would you be so kind as to let me have a few words with you.'

As soon as he saw Robby, the man smiled and said, 'Ah, young man. Now, would you like to be going to Lourdes?'

'To where?' Robby repeated with amazement.

'To Lourdes, young man. It's a town in France where Our Lady of Lourdes appeared to St Bernadette. Over a million pilgrims a year go there seeking miraculous cures.'

'That would be wonderful,' said Judith. 'But we're not Catholics.'

'That doesn't matter,' he said.

'Why have you picked Robby?' I asked.

'We've seen him around. We would like to help. There's one seat left on the plane.'

'How much will it cost?'

'Not a penny!' the man smiled. 'Children all over the country save up Green Shield Stamps. That's how most of the trip is paid.'

'I think it would be marvellous,' I said. 'When would he go?' Judith asked.

'The day after tomorrow.'

We looked at Robby.

'What do you think? Would you like to go?' I asked. He looked at David.

'Robby,' David said, 'you must go. It would be great fun.'

'Would it be possible,' Robby asked, 'to drink wine on the plane?'

'Of course,' the man said, 'why not if you like it. I'm sure God wouldn't mind.'

Robby was away for a week, and came back with a cold. But the visit broadened Robby's experience and again he was able to see others with worse problems.

'One of the priests said a strange thing to me,' Robby said. 'Just as we were coming away from the Grotto he said, "To die is gain." I don't want to die. I went hoping I could go on living, and walk.'

'That man is probably such a convinced Christian that he believes in life after death,' I said.

'He probably can't wait to die, then.'

'I don't know about that,' I said, 'but I expect the real measure of life to him is its quality and not its earthly duration.'

'You mean victory over death and *all* that,' said David.

Robby began to say his prayers once more, and with them came a gradual increase in hope, in the continued need to fight – in the will to fight and not give in. He did his exercises with renewed effort and wanted to know more about acupuncture, faith healing and all the paramedical therapies. I took him to see Harry Edwards, the 'Star Healer of the Spirit World'. His Sanctuary at Burrows Lea, near Guildford, was filled with patients from all over the world. Robby sat in front of Harry Edwards and told the ageing healer about his problems. Edwards placed his strong hands on Robby's back. Speaking cheerful words of encouragement he bent Robby's body backwards and forwards. He rotated the knees and straightened Robby's ankles – they bent back to their twisted shape as Edwards let go. This was followed by breathing treatment. Later, on the way home in the car, Robby said his spine felt better and that he could move much more freely.

When some of our friends suggested that these therapies were entirely psychosomatic, they were often surprised when we agreed with them. But if Robby could be helped by any form of treatment, using for its foundation the interaction between mind and body, so much the better.

'I remember at that time,' Robby recalls, 'how great it was to meet people who actually touched me. In the act of healing or using needles there was that physical contact. It must have been like that when Jesus touched others.'

Van Buren, Edwards, Fricker and others all impressed upon Robby the need to follow the advice given by orthodox medicine. This helped us to approach the exercises and physiotherapy with renewed vigour. One day Robby learnt about the Aura.

'Did you know, Dad,' he said to me, 'that there are rings of rays around our body which cannot be seen by the eye?' I knew which book he had been reading.

'Yes. They're known as the Auras, aren't they?'

'That's right. They change shape and colour according to the state and health of the body. Maybe they can find out about muscular dystrophy through the Aura?'

'Well, why not, Robby?'

Hope is so vital for the Duchenne boys, as well as for the world. But although hope is a good anchor, it needs something to grip. Robby could not go about being a busy, happy person without assistance most of the time, patience, understanding and the ever-present helping hands. In this situation, money is always helpful. We did not have much of it in the family, but somehow we managed to arrange holidays and go as a family. We went abroad, even with the wheelchair, and once we spent a week in Zermatt. These journeys were exhausting for us and invariably an extra strain, but we refused to give in, to give up, in our efforts to give Robby a full life. Even in the cold and snow of Zermatt, we managed to get the wheelchair by cable car to the top stage. Robby had to be carried over the turnstiles at the various stages on the way up. The Swiss cable car staff helped with the chair. One of them told Robby he was the first person in a wheelchair to go so high up the mountain.

Many people believed our efforts were directed towards our own self-destruction. They could not understand our reasons for wanting to expend so much energy on Robby. Not only energy, but also the limited amount of money at our disposal. Judith has suffered from periodic bouts of asthma since she was a child. Tension often triggers off an attack and a chest cold invariably leads to one. The strains imposed on her added to these attacks, though acupuncture gave her much relief. There was more pressure from outside our family to send Robby to a Home. As one person put it, 'That would be the best way to ease your financial, physical and mental burdens.'

'We don't look upon them as burdens,' I said.

'Maybe not – but you're showing the burden of strain.'

'We get our break when he's at Treloar.'

'That's not the point. If he was away all the time, he would get the extended type of care and attention he needs – from trained people.'

'He gets that at school, and from us.'

Care and attention by themselves are not enough. There is the greater need for love and in some ways, for dedication. We all need a cause to fight for, outside ourselves. Life with Robby is like a crusade.

One day we met an extraordinary man who insisted that life is a crusade, and everyone should face it as such. His name was Kenneth Mathew, a clergyman who claimed many successes from his healing powers. His approach was direct. He would 'lay on hands' during a normal service. The congregation took part naturally, as though they were singing another hymn or saying another prayer.

Since his visit to Lourdes, Robby had become somewhat sceptical about miracles. Both David and Robby tended to treat the phenomenon of a miracle as a humourous and unlikely event. I told them about our proposed visit to Kenneth Mathew's church.

'During the service,' I said, 'this man will come over to you and lay his hands on your head.'

'What for?' Robby asked.

'To see if your head's screwed on properly,' David said.

It took time to restore a semblance of order.

Judith came to my rescue. 'Robby,' she said, 'this man really has done some wonderful things for people.'

Robby was still giggling. 'What will happen after he's checked my head's screwed on OK?'

'Who knows?' I said.

'You think that I might be able to walk?' Robby asked.

'You never know, Robby,' Judith said.

'Gosh!' he said, and looked at David. He grinned. 'I think I'd drop dead of a heart attack if that happened!'

And he got the laughs he wanted from all of us.

We had become a happier family, and more together.

With all the tears and strain, perhaps there was more laughter and joy in ours than in many others, and the periods away from home at school were better than a Home – for all of us.

Robby's character developed without constantly being the centre of attention. His housemaster, Mr Gasston, had worked at the school for over a quarter of a century. He had the rare gift of inculcating the group spirit without supressing individuality. There was a strong sense of fairness, of fair play. Entry to the school was not determined by a bank account, but by average ability and need.

Opportunity and education can belong to anyone. But there is a need for more Treloars. For the parents, there is the freedom from the pressures, strain and constant attendance. The boy is able to be with other boys and girls, and not feel isolated. Plans have been made to combine with the Florence Treloar school for girls, thus turning it into a coeducational establishment. The sense of dedication and positive action created in Treloar in the minds and hearts of students and parents is something all schools could learn from, to help make modern living better.

Outside the school it is often difficult for anyone to understand the depth of the problems, the worries, and in particular the nature of the day-to-day stresses. Friends and associates always tend to feel pity and embarrassment. Robots and computers are often looked upon more naturally than disabled people. But the need for survival is a human problem, not only a problem for the disabled. The constant need to earn more money is also part of our society and of everyone's lives, but for the disabled, the need is greater in terms of easing the burdens. It is a heavier burden to bear for those who cannot earn enough.

Chapter Twenty-One

Lifting Robby had to be done with care, for although he was thin, there was the overall heaviness of his body, and his arms and legs could twist the wrong way. I found that to avoid serious strain to myself, I always had to bend my knees when lifting, and rise slowly with him in my arms. It was an acquired art. He could still work his trousers over his knees when dressing. Sometimes he managed to raise his arms and hold on to a bar. Praise from myself was invariably followed by a smile of pride on his face. He could still complete some operations of daily living alone and unaided. But it was impossible to leave him at home on his own. In many ways he required the same attention as a baby, but he was not in the babysitter category. There was the constant need to find people who could understand – neither to treat him as a baby, nor as a helpless individual. As Robby grew a little weaker, we renewed our efforts with Van Buren. Acupuncture was a positive part of Robby's life, but the healers' influences began to wane. Kenneth Mathew had conducted a moving service, but so far as Robby was concerned, nothing happened. There were so many forms of healing. It became impossible to try all of them. Sustaining his faith and belief was difficult in his fight against Duchenne dystrophy. Robby and his generation do not find it easy to believe. Both David and Robby were fond of the Beatles, and when the group split up, they loved to listen to John Lennon. His record, 'God', was full of disbelief in almost everything and everyone. The arguments we had were endless, and these were still a help in themselves – now more than ever, Robby needed outlets for his high spirits.

'People get help from faith and belief, Robby,' I would argue.

'Like the Jews, the Christians and all the other followers,' he would answer. 'What about the working-class hero?'

'Yes – what about him?' David joined in and strumming on his guitar they would both sing,

> *'Keep you doped with religion and sex and TV*
> *And you think you so clever and classless and free*
> *But you're still fucking peasants as far as I can see*
> *A working class hero is something to be.'*

The melody made it more difficult for me, for it was very tuneful.

'OK,' I would say, 'but there you go again, using foul language.'

At the time of Watergate, any reference to expletives was treated as an even bigger joke.

'So what are we going to do?' I asked. 'Become negative about your problems? What about places like Treloar that were founded by the kind of people who "dope you with religion"!'

That would really get things under way, but we always managed to bring these discussions to a friendly conclusion. And these arguments kept us together as a close family.

Robby once said, 'What have I done to deserve this?'

'Duchenne dystrophy is no respecter of persons, Robby,' I said. 'Things can happen to people in every walk of life. Joan Stephen in Cowfold has multiple sclerosis – has she done something to deserve that?'

'No. Not as far as I know.'

David said. 'Robby is not an old woman, like Joan.'

'An old woman!' Judith said. 'Forty-three is not old!'

'Maybe not to you,' David smiled, 'It is to us, isn't it, Robby?'

'Robby,' I said, 'the only way to escape life and its problems is never to be born.'

'Well,' he said, 'at least we wouldn't have to die, if we weren't born.'

'True,' I said, 'but think of the arguments we'd miss!' Disablement should never be a form of loneliness. Generally it is, and this leads to families being cut off from each other, from friends and even to estrangement within families. In some ways, living with a boy with Duchenne muscular dystrophy is like being in a constant state of war. A high morale, courage and self-discipline are needed to endure the constant battle. Sleep is disturbed at night for everyone. He has to be dressed, bathed and put on the lavatory. If he is not turned over at night he gets cramp. The contraction of the muscles causes them to lock. The able-bodied can jump up and down to relieve the very painful twinges. Robby has to be turned over in bed to prevent the contractures setting in. Dressing is not as simple as it sounds. He lies on his back on the bed. His limbs are lifted to get either the top or bottom parts of his clothing on. He has to be pushed everywhere. Sometimes he cannot hold a cup or cut his food.

But the positive moments can be found, must be found, whatever happens temporarily to faith or belief. There are many problems of living with each other as a family, as an individual and as a community. We are governed by rules of behaviour. Without these rules it would be difficult for a family, a group, or for society to exist. But the rules have an obligation, a limit. They are so often based on what we ought to do, and not what we must do. We must be able to overcome problems, to cherish our ability to love, and demonstrate that ability.

When Robby could no longer play the guitar, we encouraged him to play the mouth organ. When we felt that he needed more contact with able-bodied people, we solved the problem by finding PHAB, an organization for the Physically Handicapped and Able Bodied that arranged courses, events and holidays for 'PHABs' together. Another equally thoughtful body of people runs ISCF – the Inter School Christian Fellowship, who also plan holidays for students like Robby.

There will always be problems for all of us, able-bodied and disabled. Without problems we would be dead. While there is life there must be hope and positive action for everyone. Every individual needs the strength that comes from the family environment. In turn, the family needs the feeling of security and protection that comes from community life – especially those families who have Duchenne dystrophy boys. Neither individuals nor groups can endure isolation. In any human situation, it is the relationships that count the most.

Chapter Twenty-Two

Robby is now twenty and still able to use his hands. He left Treloar when he was eighteen years of age.

'I remember feeling a lot of excitement,' Robby said recently, 'and at the same time relief that I would no longer be a schoolboy.'

'But as I took you away for the last time, you said that you never thought you would be sad at leaving Treloar! But you were, remember?'

'Yes. We had that terrific last night. We smuggled a lot of booze into the house. Two blokes got sloshed, but old Gasston didn't seem to worry. Mind you, I didn't have any remorse at leaving, but on the whole I enjoyed it there, and I had no regrets.'

Treloar in many ways operated like a public school. There were privileges for some of the senior boys, which were resented by the juniors. But it was interesting how the workings of privileges produced a sense of community and not isolation. Everyone tried to help each other. And Robby was still using all his muscles one way or another. He had found it difficult to write fast, but he had been taught how to type. He had taken and passed some CSE examinations, and reached these modest objectives from his own efforts. He got considerable uplift from his intellectual endeavours. The next problem was to find a way of continuing the ongoing type of life for him. In one of his last letters from Treloar he had written, 'Yesterday I went down to the pub in my electric wheelchair, and I might do it again tonight. Have you heard anything about the Albion? I think it's time they bought another player don't you?'

'Perfidious Albion!' We could tease him kindly with such words, but we wondered if he could live for football alone? He had no doubts about it.

'If I have to die, let it be watching the Albion!' he said.

Robby is alarmingly thin but his spirit is strong. There is not much he can do for himself in terms of normal care – but he can eat, study, write, think, feel, and show kindness and consideration. Or he can behave as a demanding, bad tempered young man. In fact, he has become a fairly normal young person.

He is aware of his disease and the prognosis, but neither Robby nor the family talk about it much. It sometimes seems as though physical problems do not exist. Then the moment comes for a walk to the pub, or the journey in the car to a football match, or having a bath, or needing to go to the lavatory. Sometimes I am in a bad temper, and that makes the carrying problems difficult for him and myself. But generally, we are able to make light of those problems and joke them out of existence.

Perhaps love, and a sense of humour, imagination and realism have been of greater benefit than money in terms of Robby's life. We have always tried to regard problems as part of life, dealing with them as they are, and keeping free from prejudice and convention. An able-bodied man of Robby's age might be a less happy person. That man may already be committed to the daily treadmill of commuting and keeping up with the others in the office. As modern man's perceptions increase, so do his cravings. His dread now is his aloneness, his self-insulation. He wants assurance and peace of mind. In Robby's musings and imaginings, he often finds the answers to some of his needs. 'Let's play chess,' he will suggest, and his intellectual needs are satisfied for a while. In the competition between one brain and another there is the same excitement as that generated on a football pitch. There are the indoor games which are played with the family. The most popular is the football contest played by manipulating arms which are attached to model players. Robby's wrists are sometimes not strong enough to turn these arms.

He now finds it easier to play the electronic game on the television set. There is always another solution, another answer somewhere. 'I would like to take a girl out,' he said once.

That has not such an easy solution. But a relationship with the opposite sex can also be difficult for the able-bodied.

'Let me read you this advert, Dad,' he said.

'What's it about?' I asked.

'Listen? "Girl, many interests, seeks interesting, aware, broad-minded man, for lasting relationship."'

It was sad, but I laughed with Robby, and he went on. 'I get the most strange dreams, Dad. The wet ones I used to have are nothing on these.'

In the quiet of his bed there is sexual relief in dreams. But does he feel as rejected or lonely as the 'Girl with many interests'?

'I think life is precious, Dad. If everyone knew that their lives would end when they are twenty, they might give much more to life.'

The importance of not feeling rejected, abandoned or useless is the same for normal and disabled people alike.

'One day,' said David to us all, 'there will no longer be such a commodity as money.'

'I agree,' said Robby, 'down with money!'

'That's all very well,' Judith said, 'but we still need money to survive.'

'I suppose,' said Robby, 'money is needed for all the things to make life easier for people like me, and there certainly is never enough of it in this family.'

'We shouldn't have to depend on it to help Robby and others,' said David.

'All right,' I said, 'we needed the money to get you to the Alps last year, Robby. But you wouldn't have got there if it hadn't been for people as well.'

'What life needs is a balance,' Judith said.

'A bank balance,' Robby laughed.

The card he sent us from Mallnitz, Austria, was full of his joy at seeing the Alps in summer. 'It's terrific to see the mountains in the summer – I've got lost in my thoughts up here.' The able-bodied students looking after the severely disabled gave up part of their holidays to help. There is so much to see, to enjoy, wherever we live.

'What is important in life, Robby?' I asked him.

'To be able to walk, and the people who are blind would want to see. Some cannot hear.'

'And some cannot love,' said Judith.

'I'll tell you what's important to me,' Robby smiled, but before he could answer I quickly spoke.

'To see Brighton and Hove Albion win the Cup,' I said. 'And win the League Championship,' he added.

'They haven't a hope!' David said, and the argument continued on the merits and ambitions of football players.

Twenty-Three

The need continued for spurs and ambitions for Robby when he left Treloar. We searched and found them.

Hereward College, Coventry, is a new residential college for the further education of physically disabled young people. A fundamental aim of the college is to assist each student to achieve a high level of competence and independence. Robby got a place at Hereward. He had his own comfortable study bedroom and he was looked after by a twenty-four-hour staff. Like all the students, he became a member of the Students' Union. There are many social events which help to develop a flourishing community life. As a result of meeting at the college, a disabled man and woman fell in love with each other and got married. Robby is very mobile and is able to transport himself everywhere in an electric wheelchair. As at Treloar, there were plays, concerts and visits to the pub. But of greatest importance to Robby were the frequent visits to the Coventry football ground.

He took and passed four 'O' level subjects in his first year. His end-of-term reports had indicated that whatever the results, Robby's efforts were deserving of success. Confirmation came with these results, which also reflected great credit on his tutors and the staff at the college. We were all delighted. Such success with a Duchenne dystrophy boy also has beneficial effects on those closely associated with him.

Under the guidance of the dedicated and understanding principal, Mr A.G. McAlister, Hereward College has continued to develop the will to fight in Robby. He has learnt the need to give more to others and has made close friends in the process. One of his friends with Duchenne dystrophy who was also at Hereward, died suddenly.

'It was terrible, Dad,' Robby told me. 'One moment he seemed to be with us and then he had gone forever.'

I remembered the student well. He had smoked cigarettes, and Robby wondered if the habit had expedited death.

'Perhaps it did,' I said. 'I don't think it too wise to smoke, do you, Robby?'

The medical staff at Hereward were of the same opinion, and for a while Robby gave up smoking. He became bad tempered and irritable.

'Dad,' he said one day at home, 'I don't think I'm very nice these days, do you?'

'No worse than usual,' I smiled.

'Seriously. Do you think it might be a good idea to smoke again.'

'Robby! I gave up two years ago and you know it's still torture for me, at times!'

He looked at me very sadly.

'However,' I continued, 'if it's really getting you down – do you really think you could keep it down to five or six a day?'

'Yes. Oh yes.'

So he went back to the habit, but he keeps it to five or six a day. It makes it more difficult for me not to smoke, but at the same time, my will is tested and stretched! Might cigarette smoking expedite his death? Robby does not think about death. He does not think he will die today or tomorrow. He thinks about his studies, football – will his team be promoted to a higher division? These things matter very much to him. Within the framework of football lies the continuing spur for Robby. England have been eliminated from the world cup. Robby will have to wait another four years for the next contest – he is determined to be around then. If the potency of life is sapped by Duchenne dystrophy so that the victim's days are never fulfilled – that is tragedy. Overprotection can lead to under-fulfillment. Whilst accepting the restraints imposed on his physical life, Robby has always been afforded the means to live a full day, and perhaps with the help of football, a longer life.

The doctors say that he is going through a long period of remission, and one of them has called Robby's present condition a miracle.

One day when we were leaving the Albion football ground, Robby said that if the team had his problems they would be dead by now! 'I think I have much more fight in me than they had today,' he added. The team had lost by two goals.

'That's marvellous, Robby. That's the kind of spirit that will see you through.'

He went quickly back to his football team's defeat. 'Brighton will need a miracle to get promoted this season!' he said.

A few months later, against many forecasts, his team was promoted from the Third Division to the Second.

He once told us, 'You know, this dystrophy is so bloody and yet I've had my compensations. I might not have met you, Dad, or David, if I'd never had muscular dystrophy. I wish I didn't have the disease, but I'm glad you came into my life.'

Robby may have muscular dystrophy and be disabled, but his mind is not disabled. His inner strength has been built over the years through the relationships in our family and at school. Advice on how to develop good relationships is legion. Sometimes the latest ideas become almost as quickly obsolescent as the latest ideas in feminine fashion. But the basis is so simple – love takes over and can solve the problems. It has brought happiness to Robby and made his family better people than they might have been. Even if the doctors are proved right, he has already lived his life as fully as possible. And he has made us open our eyes to our own values and to the values of others.

During one of our discussions David said that some people think science can save us.

'Science can cure some diseases, and solve many problems. It can disprove false notions, and perhaps some conceptions about God,' I said. 'But it can't tell us how we should act, or give us the will to live.'

'What about the computer,' Robby said, 'and the man-made brain of the future?'

'Computers might be of great importance,' Judith suggested, 'but they will not teach us about values.'

'It doesn't matter anyway,' said David, giving Robby a knowing wink. 'One day the final genocide will be unleashed – a great big Atom, Nuclear, World Stars War.'

'So we might as well all give up,' Robby grinned at David. 'Only not until Brighton and Hove Albion are at the top of the First Division.'

'And England win the World Cup,' I smiled. 'Agreed,' Robby said.

Trust and respect for others are elusive qualities. Often more elusive is respect for ourselves. Respect for our lives, and for all the lives that make families and nations, is as nothing to the universe, space travel and the nuclear future. Our span of living does not matter to the universe – but for us it is our lifetime, and as long as we have it, we must live it to the fullest, and try to make the world a better place. We are all tangled in notions of right and wrong. But in the world of saving young lives there is a connectedness of values that should hold the world fully in its grip. What we want out of life needs to be balanced with what we are willing to put into it.

In the medical profession there is deep frustration for the doctors who have patients like Robby. They watch and wait for the relentless approach of an early death of a young man. But we have never accepted defeat. We have always tried to find the balance between medical diagnosis and advice, and the will to survive, by loving, by caring, and by keeping our sense of humour. And there are many dedicated people working on medical research, seeking cures for muscular dystrophy and other degenerative diseases that affect children. There are institutes, men and women, who are all trying to help by raising money, by caring.

The Muscular Dystrophy Group of Great Britain supports research projects. The money is raised by tremendous voluntary effort. Perhaps most important of all is the enthusiasm of everyone involved, from the president, Sir Richard Attenborough, down to the smallest branch in the organisation. There is the European Alliance of Muscular Dystrophy Associations, and in the USA, Jerry Lewis raises millions of dollars for the cause. The participation of so many is of enormous strength to the families of Duchenne sufferers.

There is often a sense of isolation in families with and without members suffering from disability. Mind and body are aspects of the same reality. Expressions of consciousness and the subconscious can change the chemistry of the body. A good home, a good school, a good community – these are the qualities that should matter for Duchenne dystrophy boys, for others with terminal illnesses and degenerative diseases, for all children, able-bodied and disabled. Those who cherish love of the human race, even in the humblest way, know where the responsibilities lie. The family, with its sense of dedication, love and devotion is the social unit that matters for all children. But within the framework of the family must come the schools, colleges, neighbours, friends and relations.

'What exactly is a philosopher, Dad?' Robby asked once.

David was quick to answer. 'Someone like Brian Clough,' he said.

'A philosopher,' I said, 'is a lover of wisdom.'

'Brian Clough is a wise old owl,' Robby said.

'Clough rules, does he, Robby?' David smiled.

'Not since he left the Albion. Alan Mullery rules now!' Robby laughed and went on to ask, 'How do you become a lover of wisdom?'

Robby and David were enjoying the conversation. As usual, it was impossible to talk seriously for long.

'I wonder,' said Judith, 'if any of us are wise enough to know how to become wise.'

'I think,' said David, 'that lovers of wisdom end up as lovers of their own wisdom.'

We can only discover ourselves in relation to others. The Duchenne dystrophy boy, like every child, has to be taught to think of others as well as himself, of the preciousness of every moment. The will to live can be as strong in the disabled as it is in the fittest. In fact, it is often stronger.

There is also the need for everyone to be alone at times. Robby likes to read or just sit and think. He said recently, after a quiet spell on his own, that so many people imagine life should be all sunshine.

'Why do you say that, Rob?' I asked.

'Because suffering and love seem very close to each other,' he said. 'I don't think we've lived until we've experienced them both.'

Robby's years of education have been well spent. There is a great need for more schools and colleges for the disabled, where emphasis is laid on discipline of the body and mind, coupled with freedom and independence. Young men and women like Robby need to feel independent within the limits of their capacities. The baby must be encouraged to walk in order to grow. The disabled must be encouraged to do as much as possible for themselves. The family alone would be too confined. The broad world Robby has experienced has added to his strength. Life can be fuller in fifteen or twenty years than in seventy. This means taking risks, even though they are well calculated. If we had concentrated all our attention on Robby's health, kept him indoors and given him an illusory security, we would have achieved nothing but oblivion for him – and us. Robby's experiences and relationships have made him decide whether his life is good or bad. But to win the gift of a full life has required training and discipline, love and faith, and the awakening of his power of imagination.

'I loved the beauty of the Alps,' he said on his return from the PHAB course.

'I love seeing the sea, and the Albion.' He speaks those words when we go to Brighton to watch his football team. He has learned to discern the complexities of man, on, among other places, the football pitch. The disabled have to find a source of satisfaction that is never exhausted whilst life endures. But they need to discern with the heart at the same time as with the mind. Those who have lost the capacity to find the satisfactions live emptier lives.

In wartime, the satisfactions are often found by millions, in service and sacrifice for a country or a cause. In peacetime, some find them by renunciation, or a total absorption in the service of mankind. These few know that a price has to be paid. Perhaps the other millions need some kind of national service in the world of medical or social services, to show them where their satisfactions lie. A national service to help the disabled, the old, the needy, the lonely. PHAB on a national scale.

In many ways the present has more hope in it for Robby than the beginning. He has the will to live. He keeps his heart open to the truth and the wonders that lie everywhere about us all. He is content with the satisfactions and disappointments that come and go. He fights on to survive. And it is not as lonely as it seems. All over the world the search continues for a cure for Duchenne dystrophy – for cures for all human ills. And who knows, next year his team might be at the top of the First Division of the Football League.

HUGH FRANKS

HUGH FRANKS was born in Richmond, Surrey on the 24 March 1924. He was educated at Hurstpierpoint College and later Sandhurst. He then joined his regiment – 13/18 Royal Hussars, landing on the beaches in Normandy in his tank on D-Day in 1944, he took part in the Normandy/Baltic campaign, serving as an officer in the Second World War. He was twice mentioned in despatches (award for bravery).

After the war he became an instructor and lecturer for the army and was regularly mentioned in regimental journals for his sporting achievements, and in 1949 he represented his regiment in the Army Ski Championship at St. Anton, Austria, and safely negotiated the Kandahar run.

After leaving the army he became executive director of his own successful business, then gave up business to become a professional writer.

Member of the Cavalry Club, London, The Omar Khayyam Club founded in 1892, The Squadron A Club, New York.